"In this book, Fr. O'Loughlin pulls the Eucharist out of the tabernacles and off the library shelves. He respectfully places the Body of Christ right on our kitchen tables to be shared especially with those who are rejected and underserved. He urges the reader to remember the Eucharist is not a static object of adoration but a timeless thanksgiving event where everyone has a place at the banquet table as a matter of justice. This nourishing meditation is a rejuvenating reminder that the people of God are the ones called to celebrate their own mystery of faith."

—Richard S. Vosko, author and liturgical designer

D1226234

In Christ Now Meet Both East and West

On Catholic Eucharistic Action

Thomas O'Loughlin

LITURGICAL PRESS

Collegeville, Minnesota

www.litpress.org

Cover photograph by Thomas O'Loughlin.

Photo credits:
All photographs are by Thomas O'Loughlin; except for 4/3 which was taken by Jim Corkery; 4/4 was taken by Tom Elich; and 5/2 which was taken by Richard Giles. I want to thank Jim, Tom, and Richard for making these photographs available to me, and giving me permission to use them in this book.

Scripture quotations are from New Revised Standard Version Bible: Catholic Edition © 1989, 1993 National Council of the Churches of Christ in the United States of America. Used by permission. All rights reserved worldwide.

Other translations are by the author.

1   2   3   4   5   6   7   8   9

Library of Congress Control Number: 2022943922

ISBN 978-0-8146-6875-7
ISBN 978-0-8146-6876-4 (ebook)

Occasione memoriae abhinc annos quadraginta condiscipulis meis Collegio Omnium Sanctorum opusculum dedicans.

Contents

Then people will come from east and west, and from north and south, and will eat in the kingdom of God.

—Luke 13:29

The title of this book is from the fourth verse of the hymn "In Christ There Is No East or West":

In Christ now meet both east and west, in him meet south and north. All Christly souls are joined as one throughout the whole wide earth.

(John Oxenham, 1908)

Introduction

Where Do We Start?

. . . the liturgy is the summit toward which the activity of the Church is directed; it is also the fount from which all her power flows.

—*Sacrosanctum Concilium*

Kitchen or Study?

Anyone who sits down to study a religion is struck that there are some religions that are very close to the kitchen and some that are far more comfortable in the library and the classroom. By "close to the kitchen" I mean that you have to get in among the people and what they do in their everyday lives—how they interact with one another, what special foods they eat on certain feasts, what customs are valued, what rituals are shared—to understand and appreciate their beliefs. These are the religions that tend to be studied by anthropologists and sociologists of religion, and they write books with titles such as *Ritual and Belief among the* . . . By "religions of the study" I mean those in which, over time, a massive literature—sometimes treated as a sacred canon and sometimes not—has developed, and with that a special class of learned

1

experts, theologians (though they might reject the label), who explain what the religion means, expound it, and draw ever more implications of what the religion means by reflection—thereby producing a whole body of philosophy and culture that stands alongside the religion. These tend to be studied by those whose expertise lies in cultural history, philosophy, or another theology; and their books are typically entitled: *The Intellectual World of . . .* The kitchen/study classification is a crude but simple binary that can help us get our bearings in thinking through what we are doing when we examine either our own—as in this book—or others' religion.

Over several decades I have posed this choice to groups who want to study our faith, to theology students in universities, and to potential presiders at the Eucharist in seminaries. Invariably, the first reaction of almost all is to say that Christianity is firmly a religion of the study. After all, for many the Bible is the very heart of their religion—the book of books. Even churches that are not fixated on the Bible, such as Catholicism, read from the Scriptures at every gathering. Reading, listening to sermons, teaching, catechisms, theologians, papal documents . . . the list goes on: this is "a religion of the book" and the study. Bishops, for example, are very good at writing letters telling people, sitting in rows in front of them as in a classroom, what their religion means and demands of them. It is bookish-type people rather than kitchen-type people that dominate within. Then, after many people have pointed to the evidence that Christianity is a library-based religion, someone else hints that maybe there is more of the kitchen in Christianity than we suspect. There are festivals and feasts, there are prayers at home, and some still know such customs as having holy water to sprinkle at night or when going off on a journey. Someone will then remark that their grandmother—from the old country—insisted on putting a cross on a loaf when she did some baking with her grandchildren, and, finally, one or two might acknowledge that they say grace before a family meal. But surely there is a great deal more of the kitchen than that?

Strangely, for a religious reformer within a very literate religion, Second Temple Judaism with its scriptural canon, its legal framework, and its religious experts known as scribes, Jesus never wrote a book, nor have we any of his "lecture notes" or any hint that he wrote down his ideas. The only reference to him writing is with his finger in the sand (John 8:6). His followers, such as Paul, wrote letters to make their voices present at community meetings—what were probably community meals—when they were absent, but these are not carefully worked-out treatises on the teaching of Jesus. Their most significant writings, the gospels, were written versions of oral narratives by specifically skilled people, evangelists, who traveled from group to group and who gave their performances probably at meals. We have a few homilies and a rule book on community practices (the *Didache*) but have to wait until the 150s for the first formally designed Christian book, Justin's *First Apology*, to appear. For a bookish religion, it did not get off to a good start. Then, when we look at the memories they treasured of Jesus, we see that he is most often shown teaching in meal situations. He visits houses and eats with people—and is criticized for doing so for he breaks the rules of purity:

> And as he sat at dinner in Levi's house, many tax collectors and sinners were also sitting with Jesus and his disciples—for there were many who followed him. When the scribes of the Pharisees saw that he was eating with sinners and tax collectors, they said to his disciples, "Why does he eat with tax collectors and sinners?" When Jesus heard this, he said to them, "Those who are well have no need of a physician, but those who are sick; I have come to call not the righteous but sinners." (Mark 2:15-17)

And in the climactic meal—the evening before his death—we are not told to believe or to listen and learn, but we are told to eat and drink. The central religious ritual for most of his followers is not a bible study, nor a worship service of words and music, but a meal known variously as the Eucharist, the Holy Mysteries, the Mass, or the Lord's Supper. It may not seem like a meal—but its core is a thanksgiving to God our Father before we eat and drink in the way he told us to do. Despite centuries in which Catholics hardly ever ate (for most, just once a year at Eastertime) and never drank at Mass, their officially most important duty was to be present at a meal, the *sacrum convivium* (sacred banquet), where they were told that they were to eat and drink. The center of Catholicism is located in a dining room next to a kitchen in which bread can be baked and wine prepared for drinking. Most Catholics still find that hard to imagine: the kitchen dimension seems just too "ordinary"—and that shows just how great is the challenge of the reform of our practices that began with the Second Vatican Council (1962–65). That there is such an important place for the kitchen in our book-lined religion should warn us not to confuse what we saw in our youth—or what our grandparents said they always did—with being true to what Jesus wanted.

The Bread of Life

Let me add a second story by way of introducing this book. About twenty-five years ago I was translating an early medieval Latin hymn written as a *confractorium*. Back then the breaking up of the loaf before communion in a monastery took quite some time, and, therefore, they sang hymns during this fractioning in a way similar to our singing a hymn during communion time. The hymn's words were simple, but they made no sense. I had "from the breads . . . there is [a] bread . . . and [the] bread becomes our breads . . . and [the] breads become [the] bread . . . and there is one bread . . . and that one bread is the Christ." It seemed a bit of silly repetition—playing on the various forms that the word *panis* can take in Latin: *panis*, *panes*, *panem*, *pane*, and *panibus*. I had spent my life hearing about bread in the liturgy and so knew of altar bread, technical phrases such as "a large bread" (for the priest) and "small breads" (in the ciborium), and I knew you could refer to altar bread by the thousand: "that ciborium holds 750 breads." Likewise, we all know the language of "bread and wine" as the material of the Eucharist; we sing of "gifts of bread and wine" and of "one bread, one body," and, of course, we all know the translation: "on the night he was betrayed, he himself took bread . . ." What was I missing in all this play on the word *panis*? My only clue was the echo of Paul in the linking of the Christ with "*one* bread": "Because there is one bread, we who are many are one body, for we all partake of the one bread" (1 Cor 10:17).

It was only later that day, when out walking to clear my head, that the penny dropped: sometimes the word *panis* means bread—the foodstuff that you want to distinguish from cheese or cake or custard; and sometimes *panis* refers to the actual item you bake in the oven or buy in the store or cut up to eat: a loaf, an actual loaf of bread. Since the twelfth century, most attention directed by theologians (of every shade) to the Eucharist was focused on "*whatness*": *what* was to be used and *what* not used (for example, unleavened bread, not leavened bread, was to be used); *what* was the material of the eucharist (bread) and what did it become (the Body of Christ); and *what* it then was not. With the Reformation, the "what is it" question took on a new, sharper form: what was it *after the consecration*? If that "what" question was answered "not bread," then you might be able to say you were agreeing with the Council of Trent and the notion of transubstantiation; but if that "what" question had any place for "bread" in the answer, then you were a Protestant. Not surprisingly, no one thought about translating it as "a loaf" because what was most interesting and most contested related to the *sort* of stuff that was being used. Hence, from the time that theology was first done in English (mid-sixteenth century), only one word was used in either textbooks, catechisms, or prayerbooks: "bread." And this is still the formal translation of *panis* in our liturgy.

But now think about this. From all the loaves of bread we have taken one loaf, and that loaf, being broken up, gives each of us our bread, but since our pieces of bread all come from the same loaf, we are all parts of one loaf, and that one loaf is the Christ. This is not a word game but the kernel of Paul's eucharistic Christology in the simplest words and images— and in the experience of the liturgy before the invention of little round altar breads (hosts). Now we could translate Paul thus: "because there is a single loaf of bread, we who are many are one body since we all share in that one loaf."

A loaf of bread: a diversity transformed into a more wonderful unity. Hundreds of grains (inedible to humans) are milled into thousands of specks of flour. Then it mysteriously comes alive through yeasts and is baked—transformed—into a single reality shared by those at the table.

This incident can teach us many things. First, we all tend to assume that what we are already doing and are most familiar with—perhaps since we were children—is not only "what has always been done" but is also somehow perfect. We simply could not do it any other way! But all our experience is partial and flawed: we need to refresh our understanding and our ways of celebrating. Changing the translation of *panis* from "bread" to "loaf" might seem but an insignificant trifle, but it can show us just how little we appreciate Paul and the action of breaking that is mentioned every time we celebrate: "he took a loaf . . . and broke it." We may need to change, improve, reform what we do—this was the process set in motion by the Second Vatican Council, and this process of reform will never be complete.

Second, we have a dangerous tendency to imagine that we know all we need to know within the Catholic Church about the Eucharist (and every church thinks in a similar way about its practices and beliefs), but we may have to learn from the past, from other Christians who act differently and have different emphases, and from our humanity, for we are creatures who celebrate with food and drink. It is because meals play such a key role in human life—and this was especially the case within Judaism, in which both the food and the joy of eating together were continually acknowledged as God's gifts—that the Lord Jesus was so anxious to be with us at meals. He ate with his disciples, he ate with the Pharisees (for example, Luke 14:1), and he was criticized as a drunkard (Luke 7:34) and for eating with sinners (Matt 9:10-11)—and he promised us a place at his Father's table (Matt 8:11)—so the more we appreciate our meals as human beings, the more we will have insight into his banquet.

Object or Action?

A key issue in any thinking about the Eucharist is that we think of "*the* Eucharist." We talk about it as an object; it is the *name* of some reality. So we ask, "Did you go to Mass on Sunday?" rather than, "Did you act in union with Jesus in his action of blessing and thanking the Father?" The first question seems simple, the second rotund and pompous. This is not surprising, since for most of our history we, as the people of

God, did almost nothing, and said nothing, at eucharistic celebrations. We attended, could barely hear what was said, could say not a word that was part of the official liturgy (unless one was an altar boy), and most people only "went to communion" once a year (and never from the cup). So it was a matter of watching, having beautiful surroundings that would somehow keep our minds from wandering away from religion and perhaps a choir to provide nice sound. The Eucharist became an object rather than an action. It was a noun rather than a verb. We attended it rather than celebrating our faith eucharistically.

We did not think of a loaf being broken for us to share, but of the monstrance. We thought of the Blessed Sacrament as being there "in the tabernacle," and Mass was not our communal activity. We were just the group that had happened to pick that Mass as the one to attend. But the challenge is to become the community, that one body of the Lord, which expresses itself "Through him, and with him, and in him" as loving one another and the Father, and so sharing its riches with humanity. Any renewal of ourselves as a eucharistic people involves discovering that we are called to do, to act, to be eucharistic in our communal activity as the people of God. "Eucharist" names an activity of Christians, not a something, however sacred, that they have.

Sunday, Monday

Humans have always tried to put religion in a box designated by being far from the rest of life: "the sacred" is known because it is not "the profane." This takes a popular form in the notion that Sunday is "God's day," but Monday belongs to this world and mammon. A philosopher can talk about "the mundane" and "the holy," setting up a tension between them— and between faith and the rest of life. So there is one rule for what matters (living, making money, pursuing our interests), and then religion is either a private affair or the very opposite of practical reality. We see this in liturgy: someone thinks they can address God more profoundly in Latin, but they would not dream of using Latin with their bank manager in case a mistake occurred. Another person thinks that Mass is nicer if a few performers are wearing lace and gold braid ("sixteenth-century chic") but otherwise like to think of themselves as practical "no fuss" types—in effect saying that religion has little to do with everyday life!

But Jews and Christians believe that only God is "other," all else is created. Everything, the whole shebang, depends on God. So no part of his creation can be deemed God-less, or "merely natural" or profane. For the whole of the creation— from the tiniest to the most massive, nearest to farthest—we must give thanks. Liturgy is rooted within the creation, and it is our task to sing its song to the Creator. So we have to be careful—it is a theme that will crop up time and again in these pages—about letting binaries such as holy/mundane or Sunday/Monday creep into our thinking, our celebrating, our ways of living. "Grace," as St. Thomas Aquinas said, "does not tear down, but builds upon, nature."

The Great Task

So, as creatures made in the divine image we set out on the great task of liturgy: to acknowledge and thank God our Father for all, knowing that even this desire to offer thanks is

We tend to think of the Eucharist as an object—as here in the Blessed Sacrament—and this displaces the more basic fact that Eucharist is the name of our highest Christian activity: we celebrate eucharistically. When you hear the phrase "the sacrament of the Eucharist," do you think of a group celebrating or of a monstrance? The reserved Blessed Sacrament is a sequel to our eucharistic activity rather than being its objective.

itself his gift. We set about this activity of blessing, praising, and thanking—being eucharistic to—our heavenly Father with the risen Jesus present among us. Our thankfulness cannot be separated from the recognition of our dependence, and so, empowered by the Spirit, we call on the Father for our needs and the needs of the world. But, confounding human religious expectations, this central task is not located in an awesome temple nor in a numinous otherworldly place, but in the heart of the everyday. It can happen when a group of the baptized gather at a table, their elbows jostling up against one another, as sisters and brothers, for among them, at their elbows around that table, will be the Christ.

Thus this book will approach the Eucharist from the perspective of Christianity being most definitely a religion of the kitchen—that is where our thanksgiving happens—and what we do in the study, such as reading this book, is to be seen as just a meditation upon that primary experience.

Chapter 1

The Basic Dynamic of Faith

[A]bove all bless your Maker,
  who fills you with his good gifts.
                                      —Sirach 32:13

This story, only told by Luke, might seem a strange place to begin our meditation on the Eucharist—but if you want to set what we do when we gather in its bigger setting, there is no better story in any of the gospels.

On the way to Jerusalem, Jesus was going through the region between Samaria and Galilee. As he entered a village, ten lepers approached him. Keeping their distance, they called out, saying, "Jesus, Master, have mercy on us!" When he saw them, he said to them, "Go and show yourselves to the priests." And as they went, they were made clean. Then one of them, when he saw that he was healed, turned back, praising God with a loud voice. He prostrated himself at Jesus' feet and thanked him [*eucharistón auto*]. And he was a Samaritan. Then Jesus asked, "Were not ten made clean? But the other nine, where are they? Was none of them found to return and give praise to God except this foreigner?" Then he said to him, "Get up and go on your way; your faith has made you well." (Luke 17:11-19)

We have a needy group of people and they call out for mercy—and we, the audience, are supposed to know that they have no other hope: leprosy was a slow death sentence with exclusion from the living community. Calling out to Jesus for healing is an act of desperation. We are also supposed to know that Jesus has a reputation as one who heals (Luke 5:17; 8:40) and, in particular, can cleanse lepers (Matt 8:10)—and so we hear this story as pointing to Jesus' mercy, power, and willingness to heal. And, yes, only one in ten is thankful for what he has received—but is that not the way with people: ingratitude is the way of the world!

But there is something else going on in this story—and we spot the hint of this in the final words: the one who has come back to thank Jesus is identified as a man of faith. He has not just said "thanks" but has remembered the goodness he has received; this has made him turn back. Having done so, he offers praise to God in a loud voice and thanks Jesus. The other nine are not to be found—they have not turned back and so have not given praise to God. We now see that there is, on one side, a link between turning back and looking at what one has received, appreciating what mercy has been given, and remembering where this goodness has come from. On the other hand, there is a link between being grateful and thankful and praising God in a loud voice. In Jewish theology at the time, this set of ideas was neatly expressed with two linked pairs:

MEMORY	>	THANKFULNESS
as opposed to		as opposed to
FORGETTING	>	INGRATITUDE

The righteous person, a child of the Covenant, was the one who remembered the goodness of God, and this act of recalling—turning back in reflection on what has happened to you—then makes one aware of how one is the recipient of God's bounty and so *should* lead one to praise. Prayer/praise/ the offering of thanks is a spontaneous and joyful expression of love toward God because one has recognized/realized/ recalled what one has received. We see this pattern perfectly expressed in Luke's story in the case of the returning, praising, thankful leper.

This was seen to find its continual and most simple expression in the fulfillment of the command of Deuteronomy 8:10: "You shall eat your fill and bless the LORD your God for the good land that he has given you." This was a continual call to remember and turn back to God because none of us goes for long without needing to eat—and if we can eat regularly (the great desire not just of humans but of all living beings), then we should be even more aware of God's goodness. It is also the simplest: while we may thank God for any number of gifts that are wonderful and special, without the gift of food that sustains us, the others would be useless. The person who knows that all depends on God—that God is the unique creator—is engaging in an act of remembering who they are, of their primordial origin, their dependence, their wonder, and recalling all this, their inmost being bursts out in prayerful praise. We can hear this outburst of blessing God, thanking God, praising God in this modern liturgical prayer modeled on an ancient Jewish prayer: "Blessed are you, Lord God of all creation. Through your goodness we have this loaf of bread, which is the fruit of the earth and the work of our human hands, that can become for us the Bread of Life." In this fundamental act of worship, responding to our consciousness of our situation, we notice that blessing God, thanking God—the verb that gives rise to our word "Eucharist," and praising God are not three different activities but simply verbal variations. There are three verbs but one action.

So there is a basic linkage at the heart of faith: remembering and taking stock of one's existence leads the disciple to burst out in praise and thanks. Hence Luke concludes his story with Jesus blessing that leper: "Get up and go on your way; your faith has made you well."

On the Other Hand . . .

But what of the other nine? They went off healed, and, for all we know, "lived happily ever after." But did they ever recall that they were healthy only because they had that merciful encounter, or did they forget all about it? In Jewish theology, being forgetful, not being aware of what had been given to you, was one of the roots of sin. Having forgotten God's loving deeds was the sin of their fathers (Ps 106:7). This lack of appreciation, which is what forgetting is, had led their ancestors in the desert to "exchange the glory of God" for the golden calf—"the image of an ox that eats grass" (Ps 106:20). Forgetfulness leads to sin, to idolatry, to departure from the covenant. It also produces in people the greatest hardness of heart and the very opposite of love and worship: ingratitude.

While recollection leads to a thankful community, forgetfulness produces a bunch of ingrates. The processes are imagined as operating in parallel. The more one engages in remembering (*anamnesis*), the more one appreciates, and so the greater the activity of thankfulness (*eucharistia*): here lies the basis of all eucharistic activity among the people of God. The more one ignores one's dependence on mercy, the more one lives in a state of forgetfulness, *amnesia*, and the more one moves into an ungrateful and ungracious (*acharistia*) way of life. In this way of thinking, Eucharist has an exact opposite: ungratefulness.

Remembering

For Western Christians the notion of remembering, commemoration, or referring to the Eucharist as a memorial—despite our liturgical repetition of the phrase "do this in memory of me" (see 1 Cor 11:24)—is deeply problematic. It has been the source of many disputes since the Reformation. For us, remembering is a mental activity that is focused firmly in the past. It is often linked to nostalgia—remembering how good the cookies one's mother made used to taste—and looking backward instead of forward—an attitude summed up by Henry Ford: "History is bunk!" At best, memory is just knowing—observe again that it is a head-thing—the chain of events that leads to some explanation of now: "the past is prologue." Memory can become an academic discipline as the work of historians, a marker of cultural distinction in the form of having the back-story about a work of art, or a commodity that can be retailed to tourists. But always the link between these elements is that memory is linked to the past and then is "over and done with," surviving now, in a shadowy way, as our memories in our (brains') memories. Moreover, we are often reminded that we must "live in the present," "not get bogged down in the past," and "look to tomorrow." Memories may indeed be a dangerous distraction!

This attitude toward memory is not new and is so deeply embedded in our cultures that it can be identified as one of the great intellectual chasms separating us from the world of Jesus and Second Temple Judaism. To ignore this chasm, and many have, is to fall into fundamentalism in which we imagine that the meaning of ancient actions and texts is the same as if they happened yesterday. So what sort of activity was remembering/*anamnesis* and all the Hebrew words based on the root *zkn* in the time of our Christian origins?

If we think of the way memory is used in explaining our identities—when we go back into our past to know who we are—then we see how who I am/who we are is intimately linked to the experience that "my people"/"our people" have gone through. To know me you have to have walked in my shoes! So the present and the past are, in a way, inseparable in an individual or a community. Now let us shift the image to that of an air crash investigator who needs to understand what made the airplane come down. The investigator has to go back to the very start and follow up all the clues that led to this moment: somewhere in the past being "called up" lies the solution to the present state of things. The past remembered is now the narrative that not only culminates in understanding the situation "now" (why this plane has crashed in this place) but that also illumines something larger: changes will have to be made for the future. Changing the image again, we see that "remembering" and "appreciating" are almost interchangeable verbs. To really appreciate anyone, we must think about their origins, their skills and relationships, and grasp their wealth of experience. In short, we must remember all we know about them. Likewise, a birthday party or a celebration of an anniversary is not just a "memory" of an event in the past, but the past event is a key to what we are celebrating—and the person we know and love—right now. It is because we value this person now that we want to have a historical commemoration!

So *remembering* means (for the people of the time of Jesus and for our liturgy) far more than just "looking backward;" rather, it involves *appreciating, understanding,* and *experiencing anew* today. When we speak of the Eucharist as a "memorial of the Last Supper," we do not mean a little historical drama but an activity that allows us to experience anew what the disciples at the meals of Jesus experienced, what the early communities experienced at their gatherings, and it lets us experience a taste of the future when all the disciples will be gathered from east and west and north and south at the banquet. It can be useful to translate *emén anamnesin* of 1 Corinthians 11:24 and 25 like this: "Practice this so that you all can experience my presence among you anew."

Blessing and Thanking

Amazingly, we have a tradition of the words Jesus addressed to those gathered at the table for the Last Supper, but we do not have his actual "eucharistic prayer" addressed to the Father. All that Paul says is, "after he had given thanks [*eucharistésas*]" (see 1 Cor 11:24), while Mark has "he blessed [*eulogésas*]" (14:22) and "having given thanks [*eucharistésas*]" (14:23), in which he is followed by Matthew (26:26-27), while

Luke uses only the word *eucharistésas* (22:17 and 19)—but of the actual content, the words of blessing and thanking that Jesus used, we have nothing.

This is made more confusing by the way we think of "blessing" and "thanking." We think of someone blessing something. A presbyter can bless this house or that vehicle or some religious object—it is a prayer invoking God's protection but is thought of as a kind of additional spiritual shield. A blessing is almost an object that can be given or received, as when someone recently asked me to bless a medal because its wearer "was not sure it was properly blessed." Indeed, there is a whole list of such blessings of situations (such as a pregnant woman), people (nurses, for example), or things (examples range from swords to water) that can be blessed in the Roman Ritual. The presbyter can give "his blessing," and it then somehow resides on the person or object.

Similarly, we think of "thanking" people for something good they have done, and it is simply an acknowledgement. We do know that we have to thank God—for everything—but a meditation on all those gifts for which we might say "thank you, O Lord" is not a common element in our prayers as Catholics. We are far more familiar with presenting God with a list of our needs and "praying for" this or that. Even in the liturgy, while we have the eucharistic prayer at its center, there are few of us who would spontaneously describe it as a "prayer of thanksgiving." Thinking of "the Eucharist" as an object, we are more apt to think of saying an "act of thanksgiving" afterward for having "received the Eucharist [literally: the thanksgiving]." Likewise, while in the Prayer of the Faithful we think about our needs and ask the Father to hear us, we do not have

What did Jesus bless at the Last Supper—the loaf in his hands or his Father in heaven? We are so familiar with blessing "something" that we forget that he blessed the Father and broke the loaf. This confusion even extends to the 2011 translation of Eucharistic Prayer IV, which says: "and while they were at supper, he took bread, blessed and broke it, and gave it to his disciples." The translators forgot the comma! Jesus blessed the Father, then broke what he was holding, and then "gave it to his disciples."

a moment in which we consider how we are gifted by God and then express thanks to the Father for these gifts.

However, when we turn to the Scriptures and the practices of the early churches, we find that "blessing" refers to blessing God: "Blessed are you, our Lord and God, and worthy of praise . . ." We can see this usage by noting that the phrase "Bless the Lord" occurs eighteen times in the Psalms alone. And this verb "to bless" is virtually interchangeable, as we see in the gospels, with two other verbs: "to thank" and "to praise." Blessing God, praising God, and thanking God are one and the same activity when we gather as the people of the covenant. We can see this ancient but often forgotten link in the opening words of the traditional Western eucharistic prayer: "We come to you, Father, with praise and thanksgiving . . ."

Blessing meant literally "to sound a good word for," and it has an opposite: to curse—literally, "to sound a bad word for." And this notion of a good word is what we are called to give to our Father, for not to do it is to link ourselves with those who curse God's goodness:

MEMORY	>	THANKFULNESS	>	BLESSING
as opposed to		as opposed to		as opposed to
FORGETTING	>	INGRATITUDE	>	CURSING

In the Letter of James, this relationship is put in a nutshell when he considers why God has given us tongues:

> With [our tongue] we bless the Lord and Father, and with it we curse those who are made in the likeness of God. From the same mouth come blessing and cursing. (3:9-10a)

When we say that the Eucharist is at the center of the Christian life, we have to relate it to this basic calling of giving praise and thanks to God, while turning from the rejection of those created in God's image.

Saying Grace

Few of us today regularly say grace (literally, "a word of thanks") before our meals, and even fewer say grace after meals—it is seen as one of those practices that can be construed as "practicing your piety before others in order to be seen by them" (see Matt 6:1) or somehow imposing one's vision in a multicultural society. But this hesitancy about saying grace must not prevent us from seeking to understand its significance in the liturgy and culture of the Judaism that was practiced by Jesus.

The command of the Law seems straightforward:

> You shall eat your fill and bless the LORD your God for the good land that he has given you. (Deut 8:10)

When the people of God ate, they were to bless God. But the significance was seen to lie in the fact that everyone in the land would have to do so—and since no one wants to be hungry, would want to do so—several times a day. Thus the call to bless God for his generosity, his loving kindness toward us, would be built into the rhythm of every day. We have to imagine Jesus and the early communities of disciples all having this practice as built into their lives as wearing a wristwatch is within our own. We see time and again in stories of their meals—not just at the Last Supper, but even in the miracle of the loaves and fishes: "Taking the five loaves and the two fish, he looked up to heaven, and blessed and broke the loaves" (Mark 6:41), and even in a storm at sea, Paul does not eat before giving thanks (Acts 27:35).

There were customarily two blessings—before the meal began and when it was over—and the rabbis sought to ground this practice in the phrase "You shall eat your fill" in this way. The command's first part, "You shall eat," was a reference to the grace before meals—thanking God for the gift of food; while the second part, "your fill" (or "are satisfied" or "have eaten enough"), referred to the second prayer. This prayer was thanking God for the enjoyment of the meal, the company, and the pleasure that eating around a table gives us, whether the numbers of our companions at table are great or small. Thus God was to be praised not only as the provider of our sustenance, but as the Holy One who gives us joy at our meals.

Being aware of this meal practice—a blessing of God *for* food (note: not a blessing *of* the food) and, afterward, a blessing of God *for* the company at the meal—is the key to understanding all our early Christian references to the Eucharist. It is also a key to the structures that underly liturgy still today.

Fragility

One other chasm lies between us in the developed world today and the world of the early Christians: we do not think of our fragility when we sit down to dinner. For us, food is plentiful (we are actually obese!) and at hand (we can have a take-away delivered if we do not want to have to pop down

The simplest cake reminds us that we want to share food when we celebrate. Sharing a slice of a cake like this is not about physical nourishment—food as fuel—but about that invisible reality: we are members of a community. To have a slice is to associate willingly with all that cake celebrates!

to the store). But for most societies in human history, food scarcity has been the most immediate threat to existence. Food supply is fragile. In such a situation—the human normal—being thankful for having food is not a pious afterthought. Moreover, sharing one's food is not just being sociable: it means sharing the possibility of the means of existence with others. This is sensible with one's own family—as social beings we survive in groups—and perhaps those in one's own village: but what, in a fragile world, of sharing with strangers? What of sharing with all humankind?

Chapter 2

We Are Meal-Sharing Creatures

Grace builds upon, rather than takes away from, human nature.

—Thomas Aquinas

Consider this simple fact: thinking of all the people who have ever lived, and all that men and women have done, we can see that most of their time was spent finding the food necessary for survival. In this, we are similar to every other animal on this earth: if awake, animals are seeking nourishment. Now consider another, apparently simple fact: much of that time and energy was not devoted to hunting, gathering, pasturage, or farming but to preparing food for the table through milling, refining, maturing, fermenting, and all that is connected with cooking. We are the only animals who cook our food.

Food is never just food—it is central to who we are not only as human individuals but as communities. Indeed, most of our food can be prepared only through community effort, and this reveals another fundamental truth. While believers in individualism might imagine Robinson Crusoe—"the master of all he surveyed"—as their mythic hero when he rejoiced that he had planted corn, then reaped, ground, and baked his bread, we should note that had anyone tried this, that person would have died of starvation from having expended more energy than the bread could give him! Our human food depends on human community; human community is built up through our human food habits.

Food and Power

It is often said that we are what we eat. But while it is true that without food we would die, it is also true that we are much more than what we eat. Likewise, it is clear that without human cooperation and the sharing of resources, we could not survive; and the most basic part of human working together is that which obtains foodstuffs and then prepares them for our consumption. Except in a few exceptional cases and in emergencies, we almost never eat our food completely raw: humans always process foodstuffs and then cook them. Moreover, when food is in a fit state for eating, it is then presented—this might be as simple as placing it on some form of plate—and usually arranged before we eat it. This fact of preparation, cooking, and presenting means that food cannot be separated from human culture. Food means far much more to us than simply our survival. Food for humans is about our identity; it expresses our hopes, desires, and fears, and it is significant in every human exchange.

But food is even more significant for our identity as humans: we are the only animals who process and cook our food and, therefore, need to collaborate closely in these processes, and so it constitutes us both as humans and as members of

A sign at the entrance to the college refectory in the United Theological College in Bengaluru, India. In four words it captures a basic truth known to all wise people: we learn to be human and grow as humans whenever we share food.

society. While other animals may hunt together and/or eat together, we humans are the only animals who *share* meals. It is not simply "my food" and "your food" eaten in proximity at the same time; it is *our* meal and we are participants in the human event that is far more than the total of individuals.

Meals shared mean far more to us than simply the convenience of gathering, processing, and cooking as a team. Meals are the markers of every valuable human moment: we share meals to mark our relationships, the key moments in our lives, and we bond to one another in the sharing. Uniquely, *we are meal-sharing animals.*

That we humans, and only we humans, are the meal-sharing animals is so taken for granted that we can overlook it as a fact within the creation. But if we are to attune ourselves to God, who is always and everywhere seeking to communicate his love and his vision for the creation to us humans, then taking this aspect of our creaturehood seriously is an important first step. So if we are engaged in mission—that is, bringing the light of the gospel into the dark areas of life rather than seeking recruits for our particular religion—one of the challenges is to see how God is present there before us, speaking before we speak, and acting before we act. Indeed, every group of meal-sharers—and every real human group is meal sharing—is not just engaged in an everyday (secular) or practical activity but is relating within the creation in such a way that the presence of God is at work there. Our Christian task is to help each group to discover this existing presence, and then, if they are moved to respond to this presence, to help them to imagine what they are doing and what it means, and to observe how their meal sharing may be one step on their path toward God. Put another way, our mission presupposes a common human language within which there can be a meeting between human beings; and concerns about food and meals is one of those basic human languages. This is a process that begins in meals, continues in evangelization and mission, and ends in the celebration of the Eucharist.

But before we can look at what meal sharing says about the relationship of humanity with God, we need to remind ourselves about what our own sharing of meals, and of the food that provides the material for those meals, means within our Christian memory.

Our Deep Memories of Food

Food and Trust

Food is used in the Scriptures to express Israel's trust in God—"The eyes of all look to you, / and you give them their food in due season" (Ps 145:15)—while the basic care of God is expressed in the vision that God has provided humanity with food (Gen 1:29-30). In the other creation story, they have to labor and till the ground to eat bread (Gen 3:19), so in preparing food humanity is falling in with the divine plan.

But food is precious and also precarious: famine can destroy humanity—and it can symbolize all that is destructive in human society (Rev 6:8). So the people must ask God for their food: "Truly the eye of the LORD is on those who fear him, / on those who hope in his steadfast love, / to deliver their soul from death, / and to keep them alive in famine" (Ps 33:18-19). Food is, in turn, the sign of the Father's care for each of us:

> Is there anyone among you, if your child asks for a fish, will give a snake instead of a fish? Or if the child asks for an egg, will give a scorpion? If you then, who are evil, know how to give good gifts to your children, how much more will the heavenly Father give the Holy Spirit to those who ask him! (Luke 11:11-13)

And so we pray each day: "Give us this day our daily bread."

Food and Justice

One cannot be moral and ignore the shared reality of food. The true act of worship, your "fast," is "to share your bread with the hungry" (Isa 58:7), and "if you offer your food to the hungry / and satisfy the needs of the afflicted, / then your light shall rise in the darkness / and your gloom be like the noon-day" (Isa 58:10). The righteous one "gives his bread to the hungry" (Ezek 18:7, 16), and the disciple sees the Lord in the hungry and thirsty and knows that in serving the hungry and the thirsty she/he is serving the Lord (Matt 25:34-45).

Since food is a matter of existence, any injustice relating to it—such that others do not have enough good food—is a matter of sin social and personal. The Christian is called explicitly to see that everyone has a share in the earth's riches, for otherwise some are gathering to themselves what God intends for all. In a world in which there are hundreds of millions who rise each morning hungry and where food can be weaponized in resource wars, we Christians do not need to read the story of the Rich Man and Lazarus (Luke 16:18-23) as a complex spiritual message: it shouts out to us to link faith, food, and justice as a central part of the gospel.

Food and Inclusion

One of the simplest ways to form a boundary separating those within a group from those outside it is through the use of food. If you eat *that* food, you are not one of *us*. If you are one of *us*, then you must eat only *this* food. But we have the memory of Acts 10:9-16, when a heavenly voice declared: "What God has made clean, you must not call profane." Like-wise, one can separate by having pure and impure food (and pure and impure ways of presenting food for eating) as ways of marking group boundaries. But again we have a memory of Jesus pointing out that it is not what enters a human being, but what comes out of a person, that creates impurity—thus he declares that all food is clean (Mark 7:1-23).

Nothing can declare a chasm between fellow humans like an exclusion from a table. If you are part of the "in group," then you are one of those who has a seat at the table and can eat with the rest of the group. Conversely, if you are in any doubt that you are an outsider, this will be quickly confirmed by the unwillingness of the group to have you at their table. It is not an accident that groups that desire a high degree of group loyalty, *esprit de corps*, and "group think" are those who have complex rules about who can and cannot eat with them. At the time of Jesus we find complex rules about whom Pharisees could eat with lest they compromise their desire to have purity, we find complex rules about who can and cannot eat in Qumran, and we even have the reminder in John's gospel that eating/drinking was a way of separating Jews and Samaritans (John 4:9). In stark contrast we have the example of Jesus and a willingness to eat with outsiders that was scandalous. He will sit at table with Pharisees (Luke 11:37), then with tax collectors (Luke 19:1-10), then with sinners (Luke 15:2): there seems to have been no boundaries Jesus was unwilling to break. The kingdom, and therefore its great banquet, were open to all: "Truly I tell you, the tax collectors and the prostitutes are going into the kingdom of God" (Matt 21:31).

This open commensality was a challenge to Jesus' first followers and the results were mixed. On the one hand, we find in Acts an emphasis on the meal of mission that welcomes outsiders to the table; on the other, we have disciples worrying about food and boundaries and fretting that they only want to eat with their own. Food, and our Christian manners at meals, is a constant challenge to us still today. It is far easier to repeat the early Christian slogan that God wills all to be saved (1 Tim 2:4) than to say that we are willing to share our table with the poor, the despised, and the other.

Food and Thankfulness

Our dependence on food not only parallels our dependence on God for our existence and the existence of the whole creation, as we saw in the last chapter, but is the most frequent moment when we can recognize that dependence. Knowing that we are in such a relationship of dependence becomes the starting point for all prayer: we worship God in thanking him for all his gifts—and this totality is focused in our thanksgiving for our food. The Lord brings us into being, sustains us in being, and brings our being to perfection—and we engage with this mystery when we bless God at our meals.

We find Jesus blessing the Father at table and then inviting those with him to share in a loaf and drink from a common cup—this shared meal, the meal of thanksgiving, is our core Christian ritual. When Christians have made the Eucharist into a ritual game and a source of theological argument, they have invariably lost sight of this basic fact: it is when Christians share a meal that the Lord is among them. The Anointed One is at our elbow as we sit around a common table, praising and blessing the Father for his creation and for sending us the Christ, and then as we share the common loaf and drink from the common cup.

Food in a foodbank. Food is the common possession of humanity—and we all depend on the Creator. We cannot share in the eucharistic banquet, nor understand its profundity, until we appreciate that the disciples of Jesus share their food and gifts with the hungry and needy. For Christians, liturgy and social action are in lockstep. Liturgy without social engagement is simply pretty, gnostic noise.

Meals and the Work of Jesus

But is this linking of food, meals, and Christianity something that we can say is intrinsic to Christian faith; or is it just an accident of the fact that human beings need to eat food and the simplest way to do that is to eat in common? A glance at the gospels presents us with meal sharing as a central aspect of the life of Jesus offered to us by the evangelists as intrinsic to our discipleship.

The high point of Jesus' presence among his followers is portrayed in the context of the Passover meal we call the Last Supper in all four gospels; but that is not where we should start. Let us begin with John's gospel. There the narrative begins with a marriage meal in Cana and ends with an equally wondrous meal after the resurrection, at daybreak on the shore of the Sea of Galilee, preceded by Jesus' invitation: "Come and have breakfast" (John 21:12). Meal scenes account for around a quarter of this gospel.

When we turn to the Synoptics we find the same interest. There are meals in houses, meals in the open air, stories focused on meals, such as that of the parable of the Prodigal Son (Luke 15:2-32—and note that the meal scene of the parable is a response to an objection to the commensality of Jesus), and information about meals (for example, Luke 14:9). There were scandal-giving occasions when Jesus ate with sinners and tax collectors which are announcements of the in-breaking kingdom (for example, Matt 9:10-13), and the post-resurrection meal at Emmaus (Luke 24:13-35). In all four gospels, Jesus is portrayed as present at meals and engaged in this ministry by teaching at meals. This ubiquity of meals compels us to recognize a basic fact about the Christian proclamation: it was originally heard at community meals. It was when the community gathered for a meal that they blessed the Father, "through the Christ" (*Didache* 9:2-4), and there they heard those traveling performers whose narrating of the significance of Jesus, what they referred to as "the gospel," earned for them the title of "the gospelers." Shared meals are not only at the center of human culture, but are at the center of Christian identity. Indeed, if the early churches had not gathered at meals at which letters were read aloud and performances of the memory of Jesus given by the evangelists, we might not have the collection we refer to as the New Testament. The actual new testament/covenant was performed in a community meal.

Shared Meals, Then Mission, Then Eucharist

If you have followed my argument thus far, I hope you will agree that meal sharing is something that is central to Christian discipleship not simply in an accidental way but in a positive and explicit manner. You cannot be a Christian and not be concerned with food, justice about food, sharing it, blessing God for it, and taking part with others in meals in which the Father is praised through Jesus the Christ. But food (collaborating in obtaining it) and sharing meals (rejoicing with food and making it a central element in human ritual) is a basic link with all humanity. As such, food and meal sharing can be a common ground in mission and liturgy. Meal sharing normally sets up boundaries, but for Christians it can be the basis of dialogue and welcome.

If we have a *Christian vision* of all humanity as being called by God to the great eschatological banquet, we need a corresponding *human vision* of all humanity sharing the planet's resources justly and sharing a common meal. Just as the great banquet is an image of the salvation that is God's gift, so the human meal is the vision of economic justice, ecological responsibility, and peace making that we need to work for. But we might start with some questions.

First, we need to ask questions of ourselves as Christians. Before we can use meal sharing as a common human language to dialogue over matters of ultimate concern, we need to check our own use of this language to make sure that we are not just clanging cymbals and noisy gongs. As we begin to recognize the crisis of our planet, we have to ask ourselves if we think of the creation as a network within which we collaborate—and this actually touches us when it comes to food production—or whether we look on it as a source of plunder. Similarly, we need to think of the creation as a gift—never more obvious than when we sit down together at a meal—for which we bless God, or whether we think of ourselves as masters and makers of our reality.

We make claims that God shows no partiality and loves all equally; we call other humans our sisters and brothers; and we shout about a wonderful future that is the Father's gift. If this is more than words, then we must be active campaigners for food justice—otherwise, our partiality in action betrays our proclamation as worthless.

Then we come to the witness we give in worship. Do we welcome all to the Lord's table? Sadly, many Christians use the Eucharist as a means of setting theological boundaries: can we do this and proclaim the welcome of the Christ in a credible way? Do we have the courage to challenge those fellow Christians who use the Lord's meal in this way to ask themselves basic questions about discipleship? But what of our own community? Are there those whom we would not welcome because we have an exclusive rather than an inclusive vision of Christian faith?

Second, we need to ask questions about the meals and meal rituals of those around us. In what way do those around us celebrate with food? Do they offer a prayer of thanksgiving

Gathered, crushed, transformed, and giving joy when shared as wine. The Eucharist is rooted in the earth and in our humanity; it continues in transforming us into the body of the Anointed One; and through it we come into the presence of the Father, looking forward to sharing in his gift of eternal joy.

for their food as a gift? If so, this is a basic link in faith we have in common. Do they have a sense that the enjoyment of a shared meal is either a little taste of the goodness of the universe or a basis for expressing wonder and dependence on the divine? If so, this is, at a deep level, an awareness of God's mission in the universe and in the human heart.

Not only do most religions promote domestic rituals surrounding food and sharing meals, very often with a formal religious dimension, but many take meal sharing a step further: meals become an explicit part of the group's ritual life. What does that gathering and eating together mean for them? What longings and vision of the universe does it express? A great communal meal expresses a vision of human solidarity that might be open—and so a builder of bridges—or it might be closed—and be a builder of barriers. In the very act of asking these questions and sharing with others our own Christian vision of meal sharing, we are proclaiming the gospel.

Food Security

Humans are never indifferent to food. Military experts concerned with food security demonstrate this with a cynical dictum: "Civilization is only three meals from chaos." Anyone with religious awareness sees this link between food and belief systems in the way most religions have foods that are prescribed and forbidden, times to eat and to fast, and special times with feasts. The foods that we share in our meals are not only vehicles of fats, carbohydrates, and proteins but also bearers of memory, identity, and inclusion/exclusion. Moreover, food and meal sharing is the everyday reality. Within hours of reading this, you will be involved in eating, drinking, and probably participating in a shared meal. How will you view that meal?

If I were a humanist, I might respond by saying, "We are what we eat" and think of it as simply fuel. But as a theist it is more than fuel: it is receiving the gift of God—a participation in a basic act of divine grace. As a disciple of Jesus it is a moment to join with him in a sacrifice of praise, thanking the Father for his love, and a recollection of the meals of Jesus, the meals of the church, and the final banquet. As someone called to live the gospel, it is a reminder of my duties in justice to share equally the gifts with every other human being whom I can call a sister and a brother and whom I am willing to welcome to my table.

Only when we have engaged with the human questions can we be prepared to move on to questions specific to the Eucharist. This was captured in part of the eucharistic prayer in one of our earliest Christian texts:

After you all have had enough to eat, give thanks in this way:

We give you thanks, holy Father, for your holy name which you have made to dwell in our hearts, and for the knowledge and faith and immortality which you have made known to us.

Through Jesus, your servant, to you be glory forever.

You are the mighty ruler of all who has created all for your name's sake, and you have given food and drink to human beings for their enjoyment so that they might give thanks to you. But to us, from your generosity, you have given spiritual food and drink, and life eternal, through your servant.

Above all things we give thanks to you because you are mighty: to you be glory forever.

Remember, Lord, your church, deliver her from evil, make her complete in your love, and gather her from the four winds into your kingdom you have prepared for her, for yours is the power and the glory forever.

May grace come and may this world pass away.

Hosanna to the God of David.

If anyone is holy, let him advance; if anyone is not, let him be converted.

Maranatha. Amen. (*Didache* 10)

Think again about that brilliant wall plaque. "Food shared, power released" is shorthand for a basic truth about humanity and faith. We might expand this now: whenever human beings gather for a meal, this is an occasion when the power of the Spirit is active among them.

Chapter 3

Preparing for the Banquet

Good celebrations foster and nourish faith; poor celebrations weaken and destroy faith.

—United States Bishops' Committee on Liturgy in 1972

In the first chapter, we looked at how being thankful to God for existence and for the new life given through the Christ is a basic dynamic of our lives as Christians; and, then in the second chapter, at how sharing meals is central to our lives as human beings and our memory as Christians; so now let us move on to the activity of celebrating eucharistically as a community of the baptized. The temptation is to start with theology—what it means—and then move on to what we see, touch, and do when we gather next Sunday. But that is exactly what I want to avoid. Eucharist is, primarily, our activity rather than abstract ideas about what it means. We do; then we reflect. We act; then we think about meanings.

And, therefore, any eucharistic renewal must be first and foremost a renewal in the way we carry out this activity in union with our sisters and brothers, the whole church of God, and the Lord Jesus. Experience is what matters. If we act as befits baptized human beings who are seeking to experience anew/remember as disciples of Jesus, then we shall be offering fitting worship to our heavenly Father. If we do it in a token way just because "we always did it this way," then our worship will not only not be fitting to our Christian dignity but will appear little more than mere ritual.

The liturgy is not just an assemblage of lovely theological ideas; it is a fitting and authentic action of the church. We are an assembly of people, not an assemblage of ideas.

And we live in a time when communal ritual is not a widely acclaimed value within society at large. It is also a time—the first in human history—when for most people the question of taking religion seriously or not is just one more human option. One can ignore religion by saying "I'm not religious" in the same way one can ignore football by saying "I'm not a sports fan." This attitude—that you can take religion or leave it—is a new factor in contemporary consciousness. We may reject this notion as being theologically groundless because the human heart (as Augustine said) is made for God, but it is a fact of our cultural situation. We have to take this situation as the starting point in our evangelization of ourselves and others.

This means that what we experience when we assemble has to speak to our authentic living situation and not simply recall half-remembered religious shibboleths from our long cultural memories. So, for example, a family will more likely join the assembly today because of a definite choice to want to thank God within a community than because they say "We're Catholic and that is what Catholics do on a Sunday." Our liturgy needs to chime with this new situation in which we Christians in the twenty-first century find ourselves. Why does this matter? Many people think "going to church" is about a vague nostalgia for a happy time "in the past." That may satisfy many for a partial relationship to a church building for an occasional input of ritual, but it will not build up the people of God.

Equally, we have to be aware of how those dimly remembered ideas and rituals whose basis lies in a vague nostalgia may actually be traducing the gospel we preach. Good liturgy, and authentic and good liturgical experience, matter like it has never mattered before.

Authentic Experience

So what do we mean by authentic liturgical experience? It can be thought of as three interconnected circles that give our actions a meaningful coherence. The first concerns what we actually do and experience as individuals and a community—actions. The second is the words we use to describe what we are doing as we celebrate—words. The third is our memory and desire to be a community of Christians located in a moment between the first meals of the disciples and the great heavenly banquet—tradition.

Why is this important? Every person in the gathering has been called, at their baptism, to have a place at the Lord's table. Taking part in a meal is an *action*. We are there to celebrate with and through Jesus our faith, love, and thanks toward God our Father. This is the activity of discipleship—this is why the Second Vatican Council laid such stress on the active participation of each Christian in the liturgy. While some have tried

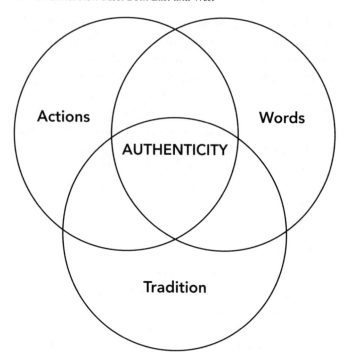

to reduce this to a kind of mental activity—and a mental activity is a real activity, as you know from reading this book—the meal of the Lord, being with others at the table, requires that we act in many ways. It demands the participation of the whole person far more than merely a disposition of interior, mental attention. Moreover, we must *understand and experience ourselves as celebrants.* We are not there as attendees or as spectators or even in the more active role of those who are fans at a concert or a football game. We are all taking part in the special, unique, and human way in which those at a table are "taking on board food," but we are also sharing a meal. The shared meal is as common as our humanity, but it is a unique experience within our humanity. Likewise with the Eucharist: we are all celebrants. The community is wholly celebrant. The best way to translate "active participation" is "wholly celebrant."

Put another way, everyone has to be as involved in this ecclesial thanksgiving meal with their baptismal family as they are with their human family at the Thanksgiving meal on the fourth Thursday of November. Eating together supposes a specific level of participation.

This is a hard idea for Catholics to take on board. People might ask, "Who said the Mass?" and people might think that it is more precise to ask, "Who celebrated the Mass?" But the correct answer is that "a community celebrated the Mass and they were presided over by Fr. X." However, taking it on board, and helping those present experience it, is a key task of the liturgical renewal begun at Vatican II. This inherent link between baptism and our having a place at the eucharistic table is why we link these in a special way in the Rite of Christian Initiation of Adults.

Words

Words are important because these give expression to what we as a community across the world, and stretching way back in time, believe about the mission that has been entrusted to us as disciples. Words, moreover, give expression, make public, what is in our hearts. Words, our words and our desire to use words, are what make us human and manifest who we are both as individuals and as communities. We dread the thought of being silenced—and we recoil in horror at the thought of not being able to speak and express our love for those around us. Words seem so simple—but where would we be without them?

We use the same words time and again so that through repetition they sink into our consciousness—but with this comes the danger that they can become just a formula, a rig-marole, that is repeated parrot-fashion, or "just words." But words matter. Words link us as humans, and they allow us to understand, to grow as disciples, and to praise our Creator. A humanity without words would be, in every sense, dumb. But if words about actions and things do not link up with those actions and things—then they lose their meaning. And when words lose meaning, they lead us to abandon them as no more than noise or to distrust them as just eyewash.

We cannot have liturgy without words; but if we have words that have lost their meaningful link to the rest of life, then we do not have liturgy. It is the Spirit who enables us to utter the words of the liturgy because it is the Spirit who gives us speech before God the Father (Gal 4:6), who gathers us and unites us and makes us a family. Many women have a sense of sorority with others or all humankind. I, a male, have a sense of fraternity with many others and see human fraternity as part of a better world. We may refer to many people in this wide human sense as sister or brother, but when we use these words in the liturgy it means far more. Then it is an expression of the links that are formed between us by the Spirit in bap-tism. The same Spirit that enables me to call on God as Father in the midst of the church, and to have a relationship with Jesus, is the Spirit who allows us to call each other brother and sister at the Eucharist. These are real words because of the Spirit's work and must be respected. Hence, confirmation—celebrating the Spirit's role in our discipleship—is the third of the sacraments of Christian Initiation.

The words of the liturgy were, for over a thousand years, hidden from most Catholics—because they were uttered not only in Latin but also in such a low voice that they could be heard only by those close by. So Catholics developed a whole parallel set of words—from the rosary to short repeated prayers to phrases that made sense to them about what they were doing. Sometimes these words took the form of images: while kneeling there in silence they just took in the glittering images on the walls. The words of the liturgy were cut off from them, but humans need words and so these substitutes were called into being by people—replacements that sometimes fitted with the Christian praise of the Father but sometimes took on strange distracting forms. For example, generations of Catholics feared that chewing the Host was a form of cannibalism. Others imagined that the reason they were not allowed to receive from the cup was because the priest alone was worthy of such an honor. Some thought that the priest washing his hands—the last visible action before the elevation—was a statement that he washed his hands of responsibility for the suffering of Jesus who was now going to be sacrificed on the cross. Yet others believed that the priest could see the infant Jesus in his hands or taste blood in the chalice. One could write several books about the ideas that were generated alongside a liturgy whose words were hidden.

Words are always with us! Once we were not respecting the actual words of the liturgy—because we would not let words that were meant to be heard by the celebrating community be heard by that community—then other words came in to fill the vacuum. Giving attention to "what the church says" never takes a more important form than in attending carefully to the words of the liturgy. It is the church saying the church's words. Again, after sixty years, the work begun by Vatican II in renewal—that of making the words of the liturgy the same words we are thinking about at liturgy—still has a long way to go.

Tradition

Tradition, for most of us, is either a boring word or it is a marketing ploy. Faced with a graduation ceremony of more than ninety minutes a few years ago, one of the graduates later remarked to the college's president (a priest) that "it was a very long Mass, Father!" His experience saw any long event with a religious element as "a Mass"! But then, apologizing for pointing out to the leader of the event that it was a bore, he added: "But I know it's not your fault, it's tradition!" Tradition here means "what is out of date but which we still have to endure." In a parallel vein, tradition means that old-fashioned stuff we still like—and we all know that nostalgia sells. Pizza is more likely to be sold as "the traditional Italian taste" even if it is made by a new start-up company using food-processing experts rather than people who have been making pizzas for centuries.

But the biggest difference between these notions of tradition and what Christians mean is that Christian tradition reaches in *both* directions. Tradition reached back into the past and reaches out, even further, into the future. Tradition is equally memory and hope. Our eucharistic gathering, here today, is but a moment in a continuum. It reaches back to the very first eucharistic meals when (as we remember them in the liturgy): "Abraham, our Father in faith" joined with "the bread and wine offered by your priest, Melchizedek." It reaches forward to the final banquet of heaven when "people will come from east and west, from north and south, and will eat in the kingdom of God" (Luke 13:29). Tradition—the active handing-on of the Good News—embraces *both* the experiencing anew of the Lord's passion *and* the foretaste of our future glory. St. Thomas Aquinas captured this double sense of tradition in his antiphon *O sacrum convivium*:

> O holy banquet in which we receive the Christ,
>   when we renew the memory of his passion [*tradition as bringing
>   the past into the present*],
>   and our minds are filled with grace [*tradition as a present event*],
>   and a taste of future glory is given us [*tradition as the present
>   preparing for the future*].

Tradition is a great river and we are always moving forward upon it. And "river" in this image is a metaphor for the living power of the Spirit among us.

This notion of tradition has become controversial in recent decades among Catholics. For many, tradition has been reduced to sticking to "the old-time religion" and is focused in the past—and even been seen as merely a function of a general attitude of conservatism. A bishop wearing the same level of court-dress (shot silk and lots of lace) as we see in portraits of

Cardinal Richelieu (1585–1642) might seek to justify his aesthetic choice by the idea of tradition, but in doing so he is ignoring that the tradition is empowered by the work of the Holy Spirit who will lead us—a future orientation—into the whole of the truth (John 16:13). A fondness for the past is one more human choice, and there are as many aesthetic preferences as flavors of ice cream, but these sentiments must not be confused with the work of the Spirit of Truth that we call tradition.

Likewise, we must not confuse tradition with repetition, as if some past moment is the perfect expression of God's will. For some Christians that past moment is the King James Bible—expressed in the car bumper sticker, "If it ain't King James, it ain't Bible." For some Catholics it means that "the Tridentine Mass is perfect." But why does the first group not stick with the original Hebrew and Greek texts? Why does the second group not stick with the forms of the second century? They think there has already been a moment of perfection! They imagine tradition as simply a pipeline from the past to the present, but it is much more than that, for it carries us forward to when we rejoice in the "one God and Father of all, who is above all and through all and in all" (Eph 4:6).

The theologian Jaroslav Pelikan summed up the confusion in this way:

> Tradition is the living faith of the dead;
> traditionalism is the dead faith of the living.
> And, I suppose I should add, it is traditionalism that gives
> tradition such a bad name.

The painter Pablo Picasso captured the same truth in a different but more powerful image: "Tradition is having a baby, not wearing your grandfather's hat." But someone replied, on hearing this statement from Picasso, that "maybe tradition is *both* wearing your grandfather's hat *and* having a baby!" This seems a nice compromise between the need to innovate and the notion that tradition is an unalterable treasure—but it misses the point about specifically *Christian* tradition. We must always give the priority to mission: to telling a new people of the wonderful gifts of God. Because mission looks to the future, to the next generation who will hear God's word and then offer praise, so liturgy looks to the future—its nature means that it is more about tomorrow than about yesterday. It is far more important that there is a new baby than that granddad's hat is still in use.

Holding the Three in Tension

Most liturgical problems arise when the tension among actions, words, and tradition is thrown out of balance.

If we say in words, "He took a loaf" because he intended to break it to share with the gathering, then it is inauthentic to take a wafer that is intended for just one person and use pre-cut altar breads.

If we say this is a prayer addressed to the Father through his Son, Jesus, but actually have actions that focus on the Eucharist as simply the presence of the Christ, with incense, long pauses, fanfares, or bells just after the words of institution, then there is a breakdown in meaning between the words of the liturgy and what is perceived as the object of the ritual.

If we are seeking to be a community of disciples on our pilgrim journey to the Father but then have some people included but others excluded, some given first-rank status and others second-rank, then this is not a modeling of the new people looking toward the coming kingdom. If we say we are sisters and brothers but act as anonymous individual consumers, then words and actions are sundered. We could multiply ex-

The familiar wafers—each a single whole made for an individual. These wafers came into use when "going to communion" was rare except for the priest; and unleavened bread had been introduced as easier to keep reserved without it going moldy. However, they speak of prepacked fast food culture. They do not allow us to experience the basic reality of sharing in a common loaf. Paul thought of one community and one loaf; these wafers signal each getting their own.

amples, but the basic message should be clear: we need to pay attention to how we celebrate as the community of faith.

We never have a perfect balance—that perfection will only come at the end of time when we will no longer need liturgy—but we must constantly strive for it. Our challenge is to try to link words, actions, and tradition in the next liturgy we celebrate. The church is always in need for further reform: *ecclesia semper reformanda*.

Confusing the Solemn with the Sacred

Anyone attending a Catholic liturgy for the first time is struck by the number of gestures, images, and items of clothing that one never sees anywhere else. Some of the leaders might be resplendent in silks with gold embroidery, straight out of a painting by Benozzo Gozzoli (1421–97). In some places you will hear bits in Latin in a nineteenth-century makeover of a late eighth-century pronunciation system, itself invented because people north of the Alps could no longer understand people from south of the Alps. It was out of date as a medium of everyday communication even then! You might hear bits of this sung in so-called Gregorian chant: a modern choir trying to reproduce an early twentieth-century reconstruction of what a medieval monastery in France might have sounded like. Then there are gestures—bowing and even genuflections—derived from the hierarchical world of the Byzantine imperial court, but now used by people who claim that they embrace human equality and democracy.

A while ago during a visit to a museum/art gallery that was located in a former palace, I found that the next room on the itinerary was what used to be the chapel. Indeed, it still was the chapel except that it had not been used for worship for several decades. It had, however, still been a chapel around 1970, for someone had added "a new altar" that was free-standing. But now it was just one more architectural/cultural exhibit. I stood there for quite a while—maybe twenty minutes—and observed the reactions of people who entered. It was so much part of the historical fabric of the palace that no one noticed that it was actually a chapel very similar to many small parish churches in that region. It was a place to admire baroque decoration rather than to pray.

Unfortunately, much of our liturgy may seem attractive not because it speaks to us of God, but because it pleases our sense of order and beauty. We assemble liturgically to be prophetic and to empower our discipleship, not to have an aesthetic experience.

Two dangers linger on the edges of Catholic worship, and indeed on that of all those churches which have a liturgy inherited from the past. First, we confuse the sacred with the solemn. While the sacred makes us aware of something beyond, the mystery that is greater than life, the solemn merely makes us aware of the big and the powerful. Second, we confuse the numinous with the aesthetic. The numinous is the awareness that life is not self-explanatory and that we are drawn outward by the Other. It is the sense that Moses was standing upon "holy ground" (Exod 3:5)—a moment in which the Creator is glimpsed within his creation. The aesthetic is firmly located within our universe and a rejoicing in what pleases us and our individual senses of "beauty." In an ideal world there might be no distinctions between the sacred/the

A space of beauty and order—with plenty to occupy the senses of those gathered while the priest celebrated the liturgy on their behalf. This is a space for an audience, rather than one intended for a community to act in union with Jesus in offering praise to the Father.

solemn/the holy/the beautiful; but given that humans beings vary, we have to be careful that a human sense of pomp and circumstance does not drown out the whispering voice of the Spirit.

But, some will cry: we have to have the past! Change is impossible! This is a frequent human response to religion, and we conflate faith with a warm sense of pious nostalgia. We behold this confusion when someone points out that a prayer in Latin "goes back to the time of St. Gregory the Great!" in the 500s. Then they insist on translating it so that one has a sense that the original Latin is elegant, rather than in a manner in which it can be easily understood. But much of this nostalgia merely tells us that the style is old, not that it is holy.

The voice of God speaks to us today in our world, just as his creative love is what upholds us in existence right now. Our God is the God of the living and of hope for tomorrow. But do we not need museums and can we not be nostalgic? Yes—have as many museums as you want and visit them. You can even choose to live close to one and spend time in it every day! But (1) do not confuse a museum with worship, and remember that (2) many people hate museums—or think of them as places where you see what is silly and out of date. Also, we need to be careful. I know lots of clergy who love visiting museums: museums seem to be their sort of place. But museums are a minority taste! Ask any parent thinking of days out with the kids: they will tell you that a little bit of a museum goes an awfully long way. Recently, I was present when a mother had this conversation with her daughter— about the daughter's reasons for not "going to Mass." "But Mum," she said, "the clothes the priest wears are just silly—it's all silly." Unwittingly, that girl had put her finger on one of the great dangers involved with all rituals inherited from previous times. Liturgy is the work of today for tomorrow, not replaying old tunes because they are familiar to us.

The *Missio Dei*

Christians believe that the human person has been created in such a way that there is a need within our being that can only find completion in a relationship with God. This is sometimes expressed by saying that "the soul is naturally Christian"—made so as to dispose it to hearing and responding to the Gospel. Another way of expressing this is with the most famous line of St. Augustine's *Confessions*: "You have made us for yourself, O Lord, and we will have restless hearts until they rest in you." Thinking about this, we could express it in yet another way: the Holy Spirit is continually moving deep in every human consciousness. It is the work of God—the divine mission—that moves us to worship. It is present in every moment in some way, and our liturgy has to give it form, and voice, and expression, and fulfillment.

The reforms of Vatican II sought to locate the table into the midst of the baptized—this reform has only half-happened, as can be seen here where there are still rows of seats arranged as in a lecture room or theater. Standing around our common table, made a family of sisters and brothers by the Spirit, we become the body of Christ, and through him, with him, and in him offer our glory and honor to the heavenly Father—and then share in his generosity.

Chapter 4

The Banquet Scene

He will show you a large room upstairs, furnished and ready. Make preparations for us there.

—Mark 14:15

We have seen in the last chapter that our experience is vital to how we relate liturgy to our pilgrims' lives as Christians: it is the *doing* of being eucharistic that speaks to us most directly both for good or ill. Therefore, looking at the basic elements of that experience can be an excellent guide to our understanding, our liturgy, and our renewal as the community of disciples.

Let us imagine this as a journey that takes place at a vigil celebration of the Eucharist, perhaps next Saturday evening, as you leave your home to travel to where you will gather with fellow disciples. This celebration is imagined taking place in the evening time—despite morning Mass having been the norm for centuries—for several reasons. This is not simply because the Jewish liturgical day began, and begins, at sundown. It is on Friday evening that the Shabbat weekly meal takes place—and this was the actual paradigm for the weekly

Eucharist on the following day, when Sunday began, among the followers of Jesus. Saturday evening links us to the meals of Jesus—he is presented in the gospels as being present at evening meals with such people as Zacchaeus (Luke 19:7), but the iconic meal of memory among his followers is an evening meal: "the Lord Jesus on the night when he was betrayed took a loaf of bread . . ." (1 Cor 11:23). The clue is in the name we give this meal: it is "the Last *Supper*"—and if we celebrate it in the evening, at *supper*time, there is a very strong, easy to feel link between what we are doing and what we are saying: "Blessed are those called to the supper of the Lamb." However, there is also a basic human reason: we tend to gather, eat and drink, and relax with our friends and family—and Jesus calls those who gather at his evening meals his friends (John 15:15) and we call each other sisters and brothers because of our baptism—in the evening. This is when we can be joyful with one another, when the day's work and its rushing are over, and we can take stock of the bigger picture of our lives. Most urban societies have their main meal, especially if it is a shared meal, in the evening—as this became the practice of the early Christians. We see this in the words used in the New Testament for the gathering: the *deipnon* (translated as *cena* in Latin), which is the main meal that was eaten in the evening. Our word "supper" is weak because it is a word now really confined to church use: the Last Supper. But think of the German for the Eucharist: *das Abendmahl*—literally, "the evening meal." We might make things more real for ourselves if we abandoned sixteenth-century English and said: "Blessed are all those people who have been called together for the Lord's evening meal."

The Shape around Us: A Household at Prayer

Now we have arrived at the gathering place—and immediately in our mind's eye we see a big, special building with possibly a spire and gothic-arched windows: we all know what a church looks like!

We so link the word "church" with a building, that it can become an icon of itself! This sign from Germany identifies a church and going to church—and indeed worship—with an activity inside a special building. This linking of religion with specific buildings is deep within our memories: but the risen Christ is present in the whole of the creation. There is no unholy place since God is the Creator of all.

But take note of this simple statement by Paul: "[W]hen you come together as a church . . . " (1 Cor 11:18). We do not gather *in* a church, we gather *as* a church. Here lies one of the great misdirections in Christian life today: we think of a building or an organization when we hear the word "church"; we forget that it is the name of who we are when we celebrate the Eucharist. There is a joke told about a bishop at Vatican II who had a minimal command of Latin. He kept hearing discussions on the church (*ecclesia*) and its structure. Annoyed that the discussion was going on for so long, he remarked that he wished someone would decide on the design (structure) and build this church—then they could discuss something else! We are all more like that bishop than we think! Our culture is based on consumerism: I go to a common point to get something for myself; if there are others there at the same time, then the group is simply "a crowd." Sadly, we tend not to think of the assembly for the Eucharist as a single reality, church, of which individuals, you or I, are parts. We default to thinking of "going to Mass and getting Holy Communion"— a private and personal thing—and we hope the church (a building—the sacred equivalent of a service station or shop) will not be too crowded!

Back in the 1920s, the German theologian Romano Guardini was so worried about people confusing being a church with the building that he had people assemble for the Eucharist in a great empty, white hall, without any special religious codes—such as pointed windows or stained glass—or any distractions such as sets of paintings (originally put there to keep people's minds occupied with pious thoughts while the official liturgy took place in silence at one end of the building)—so that the group would realize that it was they, themselves, the group, that was the church.

Our focus is upon ourselves as a family gathering of brothers and sisters—the people of God—for we are not alone: among us, present when we assemble, is Jesus. "[T]ruly I tell you . . . where two or three are gathered in my name, I am there among them" (Matt 18:19-20). We have gathered in his name, we are his body.

Sadly, it is often very hard to feel this sense of being together. Many of our older churches were designed with an individualist spirituality in mind, many love the distractions and are so fascinated by lots of statues that they do not think

A sign outside a small building in Wales: what it lacks in typographical sophistication is more than made up for in theological precision. The church is the gathering, the building is but a shelter from the weather.

about the community. Some have even returned to a décor that looks so "otherworldly" that we forget that liturgy takes place in our world—the world in which the Son of God took flesh. Other people become so focused on the Blessed Sacrament in the tabernacle that they forget that the community is the primary sacrament: we are the body of the Christ. Our renewal in the form of concentrating on the assembled body of disciples, begun at Vatican II, has a long way to go—and cuts at both a popular aesthetic of the "ethereal is spiritual" (an aesthetic that runs counter to the incarnation) and the notion that religion is an individual affair (which forgets that God's call is for each of us to become a part of the body of the Christ: the community of the baptized).

In effect, the building is just a wraparound—to keep out the weather and allow us to be comfortable as a group—and we, the assembly, are what it is about. So do we not need beautiful church buildings? Yes—they have uses and are good as places for private prayer, but we no longer need them to give us something to think about while the liturgy takes place. We are all now participants—and if a building interests us more than what the community is doing, then that building has failed as a place for our celebrating.

The Location: A Table Set among Us

So do we have a focus when we assemble? We are called to share at the Lord's table, and our being at this table is a memory of the tables in our past and an anticipation of the heavenly table. It is a table—that familiar everyday object—that is the focus of our banquet.

Here we run into a bit of historical confusion, for it has become commonplace to refer to the central object of any church-building as "the altar." We Catholics might have several altars in one building (the high altar and the side altars), but we are pretty certain what we mean by the word "altar"—it is where the priest says Mass. The situation is anything but clear, however! In the ancient world every temple had an altar, and this was the place the specially appointed people—priests—carried out their rituals for the people. This language was also used, when writing in Greek, by Jews so that they could explain the temple in Jerusalem to the larger world, but we should note that the altar in Jerusalem at which the morning and evening sacrifices of praise were offered was actually conceived as the Lord's table: there Israel offered him food each day. Back in the Gentile world there were other altars: domestic-size ones on which a family made its offering to the gods of the household. Every well-off home had such an altar, and even the poor could consider the fireplace (the "focus") as an altar for sacrifices (usually bits of food or a splash of wine poured out for the gods) to the gods who brought good fortune to those offering.

Needless to say, this sort of religion was seen as superstition by Jews (and then by Christians) and was rejected. Hence, the early third-century Christian apologist Minucius Felix repeatedly says, "the Christians have neither sacred groves nor altars"—it is silliness to think that such practices could influence the God of goodness who sustains the universe. But, and it is a very big "but," most Christians who were Gentile in origin had such an attachment to the language and ideas of altars and pagan sacrifice that they carried this culture into their

Christianity. And with large groups becoming Christian—once it was "the done thing"—the simplest way to explain the new religion was to parallel it as closely as possible with what was already familiar. So the leaders of the community (presbyters) became priests (*sacerdotes*), the buildings for their meetings became their temples (sometimes the very same buildings continued in use with some adaptation: in Rome, the Pantheon—to all the gods—became *Sancta Maria ad martyres* [*Santa Maria Rotondo*]); and the tables of the Christian gathering became their "altars." This confusion can be seen in the shapes of the objects. The object in Christian buildings is

Sta Maria Rotondo, once the Pantheon, in Rome. As temples became churches, most of the devotees continued to think about what was happening in the building in the much the same way.

always shaped somewhat like a table, but no pagan altar has that shape—they look more like a small box; but we call both of them altars. Perhaps more importantly, many religious attitudes that belonged to the world of the pagan altar also continued among us: have you ever heard of anyone "having a Mass said" to help obtain a favor from God? Old, bad theology dies hard!

But Jesus located his action of a loving sacrifice of praise to the Father not in a numinous special "other" location, but in the heart of human community: in the household around the table. The household table—already a holy place within Judaism for the weekly Shabbat meal, the special meals on feasts such as Pentecost (Shavuot), and most especially for Passover (Pesach)—would be the place of memory, petition, and praise. His disciples would be characterized by that loving intimacy that goes with a common table, and their prayer would be characterized by their thankfulness to the Father for his daily goodness to them.

The table—any table at which we have a place—is a place and marker of identity: you may sit here. It is also a place of welcome—you can sit with us and share our food—so that no one is a stranger. The table is our image of hospitality and generosity—heaped high with good things for a feast—and speaks to us both of the hospitality of God who alone is wholly generous and reminds us of our need to offer generosity and hospitality: "I was hungry and you gave me food, I was thirsty and you gave me something to drink" (Matt 25:35). But the table is not only the welcome of God for each of us and of each of us for each other, a common table speaks to us of equality and dignity—we do not have a "high table" or a "top table" or a "servants' table" or a "poor persons' table" (this was Paul's criticism of the Corinthians)—but gather as those reborn in baptism. However, most of all, the table is part of our lives with those who are nearest and dearest to us: the family table is the idealized place of our communal happiness—and that table is extended to our family in baptism. We gather around it as sisters and brothers, rubbing shoulders with one another, rubbing shoulders with Jesus present at this table. To stand around the eucharistic table is to have the Lord Jesus at our elbow.

Gathering around the table was the rationale for the architectural changes after Vatican II—the altar was not to be at one end, near a wall, as was prescribed for altars in Roman temples by the pagan architectural writer Vitruvius—but to be a table set in the midst of the community. Because the table is in the midst of the baptized, Vatican II saw the Lord's table as a symbol of the presence of the Christ in the midst of the assembly—and ordered the changes in our buildings. This has not really gone well in practice. In many places, the reason for the change was misunderstood; it was assumed it was a matter of visibility so that people could see the priest more easily. So the table was pulled out from the back wall as if it were the teacher's desk for demonstrating an experiment in chemistry! Those who did this minimal change forgot that we do not attend/watch/or have Mass said for us, but we—all who are called to the Lord's table—all are celebrating: it is our meal, our table, our thanksgiving sacrifice.

This is not a new idea but is even found in the words of the First Eucharistic Prayer (the Roman Canon) in these words:

Memento, Domine, famulorum famularumque tuarum,
et omnium circumstantium,
quorum tibi fides cognita est et nota devotio . . .

Literally, this translates like this: "Recall, O Lord, your male household servants and your female household servants, indeed all who are standing around, whose faith is known to you and their devotion is clear . . ." We are the *circumstantes* at the Eucharist, those who stand around the table: it is our place.

It is a good idea to watch how people behave at tables. If there are just two of us—even if it is just for coffee—we will

Sts. Peter and Paul, Bulimba, Brisbane. An early twentieth-century building has been remodeled so that (1) the table is in the middle of the assembly; (2) the Word of God has a place of honor with the ambo also set in the midst of the gathered disciples; and (3) the baptismal font is at the place of entry into the church/community.

sit opposite each other at a table so that we can see each other's faces. If four of us, then we might each take one side of a table. If slightly more are present, we might have a round table, which gives us as much interaction as possible. We can be very sensitive to where we are placed at a table as in this bit of gospel wisdom: "But when you are invited, go and sit down at the lowest place, so that when your host comes, he may say to you, 'Friend, move up higher'; then you will be honored in the presence of all who sit at the table with you" (Luke 14:10). And places at table in the assembly among the early followers of Jesus led to a warning in the Letter of James about those who give better seats to the wealthy and well dressed and lower seats to the poor (Jas 2:3)—the table is the table of those valued in God's sight rather than in ours. Appreciating how tables function in our everyday lives can give us a deeper awareness of who we are as a eucharistic community. Appreciating that our central cultic space is at one with our central family space can give us a deeper awareness of the closeness of the incarnate Son in our everyday lives. Appreciating the generosity of the Lord's table can serve us as a model for our generosity with the earth's bounty toward our fellow humans. And appreciating our common table as we stand around it can remind us of our vocation: to recline at the table in the kingdom of God (Luke 13:29).

Let's Sit Down Together

However, in most of the buildings intended for liturgy, across the Christian spectrum, you will not be around the table but will sit on a bench in an auditorium. The situation is closer to that of being in a big classroom or school hall. The locale is designed so that you can watch (a Catholic emphasis), listen (a Protestant emphasis) to what is taking place on the altar (a Catholic emphasis) or in the pulpit (a Protestant emphasis). Indeed, many think of worship primarily in terms of a school-room: hear readings, sing hymns, listen to a sermon—and perhaps there are items after that such as Holy Communion. Here lies the inherited confusion—in all traditions—of centuries. Unpicking it is difficult!

The meals of any group in the ancient world had some sort of entertainment during the meal, such as singing or a recitation of poetry or a special speaker who read some portion of an epic. Similarly, the Passover meal had recitations from the Scriptures. So when the early communities of Jesus' followers gathered—and that was invariably for meals—they performed texts that recalled their history and identified them as God's people. Moreover, there were teachers who traveled among the churches—we know only a handful of names, but Paul is the most famous—who gave their teaching at these meals. One of the great needs of these communities was to hear the words of Jesus, and a special kind of traveling teacher emerged who was valued for just this sort of performance: an evangelist. An evangelist was one who could recite the memory of the words and deeds of Jesus. We know that there were many of these evangelists (Luke 1:1-3), and some not only gave live performances—it was an oral culture—but left a "recording" that could be revoiced at other community meals when no evangelist was present. Out of this group, four recordings became, first, very common, and then special, and then, by the later second century, normative. Thus we have the gospels of

Matthew, Mark, Luke, and John. The name of the book, "gospel," is derived from the name of the kind of teacher who originally performed its contents live: a "gospeler" (evangelist). When we take extracts from these and revoice them on Sunday, we are continuing this ancient practice. They are not really readings—this is a word belonging to book culture—so much as the replaying of recordings of four individuals' "take" on the significance of the risen Jesus. It was to tune into this fundamental fact that Vatican II wanted a new lectionary. The old lectionary concentrated on just Matthew, while our new lectionary looks at the whole range of the gospels over three years.

But the communities knew that they could only understand this risen Jesus "according to the scriptures" (that is, what we call the Old Testament), and so this, too, was read at their meals. Likewise, others (most famously Paul) had written letters to the churches—remember that a church is an assembly at a meal—and so these, too, were read again and again. But readings were interspersed with hymns and psalms: group singing on what was a joyous occasion. Thus we see how our Liturgy of the Word emerged.

Several centuries later, this whole part of the eucharistic gathering became opaque to the majority as it continued to be performed in Latin, but first the Irish and then the Germans could not understand it. Later again, with the rise of the romance languages (Spanish, Italian, and French dialects), it became a silent event except in monasteries. Now, to fill the gap, the sermon arose—a short, didactic lecture (as distinct from a homily, which is an interpretation of the readings), and the emphasis shifted from reflection to moral exhortation.

And even sermons were few and far between outside urban churches run by the religious orders such as the Dominicans and Franciscans.

With the Reformation, with its focus on hearing the Bible, preaching the Word of God, and hymnody as worship, this became the very center of liturgy, and has remained so in many Protestant churches. So the pulpit became the central location, and bench seating (as best suited to listening to words from a speaker) filled the nave. Soon Catholics, not to be outdone, also took to bench seating and the pulpit oratory became a central liturgical form, especially with such orders as the Jesuits and the Redemptorists. The great "hell and damnation" sermon—the "scare them into righteousness" approach—had become the hallmark of Western Christian instruction. Alas, both among Catholics and Protestants, this ministry of the Word (readings and sermon) was not seen as having any intrinsic link to the celebration of the Eucharist—and so it took off to have a life of its own as the cornerstone of Protestant worship and as evening "missions" and "devotions" among Catholics.

Vatican II has sought to restore the link: when we gather we recall, remember, experience anew the words of the Lord. Hence we say that Jesus is present in the readings—all of them—and that we hear his voice in the revoicing of the gospels. The words of the presider, far from being a lecture or a moral diatribe, are to try to help us take these ancient texts and see their stories as part of our core religious identity. It is in reflective remembering that we discover who we are, hear the Lord's voice, and come into the presence of Jesus who today is fulfilling the Father's will among us: then Jesus rolled up the scroll, returned it to the man in charge, and sat down. And he began by saying, "Today this scripture has been fulfilled in your hearing" (Luke 4:20-21).

It is because the Christ is present in the Liturgy of the Word that the ambo—from which the Scriptures are proclaimed—is far more significant to us than a pulpit or lectern or podium. The ambo is located among us, for from it we hear within us the Word of the Lord.

For this sort of meditative recollection which leads to praise and prayer, the inherited lecture-room format is far from ideal—it presupposes the old "filling an empty vessel from a pitcher" model of learning. But we are the people of God, and we need to hear both the Scriptures and what the Spirit is saying within each of us. We are there to encounter the living God rather than to get an expert's lecture, and for this an arrangement of seats around our table is far more useful. This is a truth we all know from small groups, meeting where we need to reflect and share, and teachers know that the old format of rows of desks (the parallel of church benches) is not conducive to an internalizing of what we are talking about. The reform begun in 1969 with the new lectionary has barely begun in many places.

Let's Stand!

Some rituals are so simple that they pass us by! A case is point is that we stand together when we make requests of God during the Prayer of the Faithful in the assembly. The interesting thing to note is that it is not just a string of petitions simply bunched into one place for neatness: it is not the *Prayers* (note the plural) of the Faithful, but the *Prayer*. It is part of the task of the people of God to voice its needs, the needs of the community, and the needs of humanity before God. Voicing our needs is not the same as giving God information, nor is it equivalent to bothering God in the hope that more and more noise might move God to action! Voicing our needs is an acknowledgement of where we are as needy creatures, a declaration of our dependence on God, and a confession that the answer to the world's problems is greater than the creation.

The curious thing is that when we exhibit our neediness we do not grovel, nor kneel, but *stand*. In this we are following an ancient bit of ritual practice. Jesus' first followers stood in the synagogue when praying (Matt 6:5). A generation or two later, when they gathered they still stood to pray because Mark (11:25) puts this into the mouth of Jesus: "Whenever you stand praying, forgive, if you have anything against anyone; so that your Father in heaven may also forgive you your trespasses." And a generation later again, another teacher wishes "that . . . intercessions, and thanksgivings be made for everyone . . . [and] that in every place the [people] should pray, lifting up holy hands" (1 Tim 2:1, 8).

Standing together praying is a statement that all the baptized are the priests of the new covenant.

The Basic Stuff: A Loaf of Real Bread

One of the strangest aspects of all the canonical accounts of the Last Supper, from our perspective, is that when they tell us that Jesus blessed/thanked the Father, they do not give us the words of that blessing! That blessing was his eucharistic prayer, his words thanking God, yet they are not even hinted at. The text—already an item on teaching before Paul wrote in 58 CE—is typical: "then when he had given thanks, he broke it." Would we not love to know the eucharistic words he used?

The reason for this silence is not hard to find. When we look at another first-century Christian text, the *Didache*, we find a eucharistic prayer and it follows the pattern of standard Jewish table prayers, with the addition of "through the Christ, who is our Lord." What was distinctive—and so to be remembered by his followers—were not his words of thanksgiving but his actions.

The most distinctive element was that he took a loaf of bread, said the blessing, and then gave each of them a piece of his own loaf. This action—focused on *the form of a loaf* rather than a particular kind of food (bread) is at the heart of what we do.

Indeed, at least until the ninth century in the West we did this, at least in monasteries, since in ordinary parishes ever fewer "went to communion," but when it became the norm for only the presider to eat, the loaf shrank in size to being just big enough for one person. It was still broken, but this was just a gesture, since it was not shared and the priest ate both halves. Moreover, with few if any "going to communion" and ever more interest in the Blessed Sacrament, there was a shift from living bread (still used in the Orthodox and other Eastern churches) to unleavened bread, which did not go moldy in pyxes (literally, a box, what came to be called tabernacles in the sixteenth century). Then scholastic theology gradually descended into focusing on "substance"—what is it: a material called bread—and missed the significance of Jesus' action. Then once we started to translate *panis* as "bread"—the usual form in most modern translations of both the liturgy and the Scriptures among both Catholics and Protestants—the focus of the liturgy's key action became virtually invisible.

It is only when we actually have a loaf of real bread, then break it so that a piece can be held by everyone in the assembly, that we can reflect on what is said about this in the Scriptures. We are the body of the Christ, we are the beneficiaries of his sacrifice, we are one with him, we are the scattered children of God that have been regathered like the grains of wheat and transformed by him and now stand in the presence of the Father.

Alas, we have, over centuries, become so dull and insensitive to this fundamental action of the Eucharist that many Catholics, even presbyters, cannot see what all the fuss is about. So, we still have places in which there is a large bread for the presider alone—he breaks this, but this is a physical action without experiential consequences and so is meaningless. I have heard priests say that they imagined the reason for breaking it was simply to make it more comfortable for them to consume! Then there are private, individualistic small breads in a ciborium: this precut-for-easy-distribution approach is based on the logic of a fast-food counter rather than on the logic of a fundamentally distinct Christian action. We even see the tabernacle used at celebrations of the Eucharist as if sharing the one loaf which is the Christ (1 Cor 10:17) is equivalent to having a store of a commodity. If you go to a meal, you expect to eat the food of that meal—not yesterday's! Such practices are not only a source of a confused understanding of what we do as disciples, but they also make the whole of our liturgy seem little more than nice words that do not match up with reality.

The Shocking Action: A Shared Cup

Sharing a loaf may be awkward and slow down the ceremony—a basic liturgical fault for many people—but it is relatively simple and, indeed, we regularly cut up a loaf so that people around a table can have a slice, and we are also familiar with domestic rituals such as sharing slices of someone's birthday cake. So, although it is slow, many people think a real loaf and real fraction could be a liturgical improvement. But the second action of Jesus is not nearly so neat—indeed, it is wholly countercultural.

We may be willing to share anything that is put into the center of a table (such as a basket of bread), but we drink liquids from our individual cups. We may go for a cup of coffee with one another, but we expect that we will have as many actual cups as people. We may share a bottle of wine, but we will have many glasses. Only when we observe the virtually universal fact that we drink liquids from separate vessels can we recognize that Jesus' distinctive action was that his table companions shared not a liquid but a cup.

While our common memory of the origin of the Eucharist in the Last Supper is that Jesus took bread and wine (a recollection that emphasizes the distinct materials), by contrast, all our early texts notice that he took a "cup" (for example, see 1 Cor 10:16 and 21). And that it was filled with wine is then inferred from a subsequent statement found in the Synoptic tradition: "Truly I tell you, I will never again drink of the fruit of the vine until that day when I drink it new in the kingdom of God" (Mark 14:25; see also parallels Matt 26:29 and Luke 22:18). But is this early usage of a cup (and, therefore, the manner in which that drinking took place), when contrasted with the later emphasis on the cup's contents (hence, on what was consumed), of any real significance? Put another way, is seeing a specific reason for the mention of a "cup" anything more than a curiosity?

That this is important can be seen in a variety of ways. The most obvious evidence that a cup was significant in the churches' memory was that having taken the cup and blessed the Father, Jesus gave it to those at table so that they each drank from it. It was not that they all drank wine, or any other liquid, which they could do from their individual cups, nor that they all had a drink of the same wine in that it came from one source, such as a flagon, but that they passed a cup from one to another and *each drank from that same cup*. When we recognize this, we see at once that the cup was at least as significant to them as what it contained. The focus of early memory was on the how of their drinking, not upon *what* they drank.

As a start, we need to recognize just how unusual was this action of sharing a drinking vessel. There was no equivalent to it in any known Jewish practice such as Sabbath or Passover meals, there is no mention of anything like it in any other Jewish sect, nor are there any literary references to such a practice either in Jewish documents that are certainly earlier than Jesus (be they canonical or not), roughly contemporary with him (for example, in Philo or Josephus), nor those later than him which might point to earlier times (for example, the Mishnah). *Making the sharing of a cup part of one's table manners is confined exclusively to the followers of Jesus.*

The traditional "chalice" (literally calix *means a stemmed cup) is more akin to an individual's wine glass than to a cup intended to be shared by a community. The drinking vessel on the right (the gospels use the word* potérion, *which is akin to our common word: "cup") holds 600 milliliters. Some early medieval cups (such as the Ardagh Chalice from Ireland) hold 1½ liters and have handles to enable them to be passed with greater ease.*

That it was the action of sharing one cup that was central (rather than drinking from a common volume of wine) is seen indirectly from the second- and third-century evidence when uniformity between the churches was becoming more important. One of the practices that came under criticism was that of sharing a cup of *water* at the Eucharist. This practice was both widespread and deep-rooted, and it cannot be dismissed as some sort of later-developing deviation. Using water probably avoided disputes over the interaction of rich and poor, the problem of cost, and between those happy to drink wine and those who suspected the practice (such as former disciples of John the Baptist). But when later bishops wrote about the practice, they did not deny the reality of those eucharists but stressed the better practice of using wine. The implication is that they recognized that sharing of a common cup was fundamental.

Are there any traces of how this most unusual gesture was understood? Clearly, by parallel with the sharing of portions of the loaf, a key element in the significance of the shared cup may have been the unity of the participants at the gathering with one another and with the risen Lord. If sharing a loaf indicated the intimacy of the table and the unity of those around it, then the level of intimacy of passing a cup around the table is even greater. However, hints linking the cup to the unity of the community are not found in our earliest sources. In the *Didache*, in which the unity of the community and the work of Jesus in gathering it are presented by analogy with grains that formed the loaf, we do not find any parallel notion such as that of individual grapes being combined to form wine—a parallel focusing on the cup's *content* rather than its *sharing*. Likewise, Paul points out that "[b]ecause there is one loaf, we who are many are one body, for we all partake of the one loaf" (1 Cor 10:17 [note Paul assumes a single object, a loaf, so the NRSV has been changed here from "bread"]), but there is no parallel statement about sharing the cup. For Paul the choice facing those who share the cup is between "the cup of the Lord and the cup of demons. You cannot partake of the table of the Lord and the table of demons" (10:21). This choice between the Christ and the demons was a choice that faced all Gentile disciples: were they willing to turn from the idols that were part of the social and domestic fabric of Greco-Roman urban life? If one wanted to express the new discipleship, then one not only turned from that which had been offered to idols, but one partook of the common cup of the disciples of the Christ. Drinking from the common cup was a boundary ritual that expressed commitment to discipleship, and as such it was a serious matter and they would have to answer for their decision to drink from that common cup (11:27-28). Since it is the action of declaring both commitment to discipleship and rejection of idols, it is a participation in the life-blood of the Christ (10:16) and makes them part of the new covenant that was sealed in Christ's blood (11:25). For Paul, discipleship is about being part of the new covenant and sharing in the new life offered by the Christ; and taking the common cup—not a gesture done lightly—was accepting that discipleship and taking that life-blood of the Christ into one's own body. We are accustomed to think of the act of baptism as *the* boundary ritual of the new community, but for Paul, at the time he first wrote to the Corinthians, the sharing of the cup was also a demarcation ritual—and since it was repeated weekly it was the ongoing declaration of willingness to continue along the Way. That such a paralleling of drinking the cup with baptism was present in Paul's mind when he wrote about that church's meals is confirmed by his remark about the Spirit being present in that church: "For in the one Spirit we were all baptized into one body—Jews or Greeks, slaves or free—and we were all made to drink of one Spirit" (12:13). Just as the Spirit united them in baptism, so the Spirit was now what they drank in common. In short, if they wanted to be part of the new people, then they drank from the common cup, accepting the consequences.

The assumption of the *Didache* is that those who are eating at the meal have already made a choice between the "Way of Life" and the "Way of Death"; and it is explicit that only those who are baptized are to eat and drink (9:5)—so willingness to eat from the loaf and drink the one cup are marks of continuing commitment. This relationship between baptism and drinking as boundaries may seem strange to us who put these sacraments into different theological compartments: one is about joining and a one-off event, while the other is about continuing and is repeated over a lifetime. However, such a neat system of outcomes does not fit with how ritual establishes and maintains identity. One-off events need to be constantly recalled, while that which is an ongoing concern needs to be seen to have a moment of establishment. They were living as disciples—day by day facing the challenges of discipleship— and so they declared themselves day by day while looking back to the moment when discipleship was established. The two rituals, baptism and drinking the common cup, need to be seen as complementary within living a life of commitment, rather than as distinct from each other with different functions in a theological system.

Looking at the Synoptic tradition, we see that this notion that the one cup of the Lord is to be understood as willingness to accept all that discipleship involves is reinforced, while being given a narrative expression, within a paradigm encounter of would-be disciples with Jesus. The scene appears in Mark 10:35-40, where James and John, the sons of Zebedee, ask if they can sit beside Jesus in glory. This prompts a challenge that links drinking the same cup as the Lord with baptism: "Are you able to drink the cup that I drink, or be baptized with the baptism that I am baptized with?" (10:38). When they reply that they are able, they are told, "The cup that I drink you will drink; and with the baptism with which I am baptized, you will be baptized" (10:39), but that will not guarantee them their desired places. To accept fully what it is to be a disciple is both to share in the baptism of Jesus and to drink the same cup as him. In Matthew 20:20-23 the story reappears, but now the question is asked by their mother and the reference to baptism has disappeared, but the message is just as stark: to be a disciple means drinking from the same cup that Jesus drinks—and this invites from the audience a ritual conversion: if you drink the ritual cup, then you consciously declare your readiness to accept the cost of discipleship.

This theme linking the drinking of the cup with discipleship is further developed in that Jesus' own discipleship to the Father is presented as his willingness to drink the cup that the Father offers him. In both the Synoptics and John, the suffering to be undergone by the Father's Anointed is presented in terms of his "cup" and Jesus' willingness to drink it. In Mark 14:36, followed closely by Matthew 26:39 and Luke 22:42, this is presented as part of his prayer in the garden: "Abba, Father, for you all things are possible; remove this cup from me; yet, not what I want, but what you want." And thus with obedience he accepts where his discipleship has led. In John 18:11 Jesus is presented as doing the Father's will without hesitation or any sign of human fear, but again he is drinking "the cup" that the Father has given him.

Drinking from one cup was a declaration of acceptance of a common community destiny and a common destiny with the Christ. As such it formed a very real, and possibly physically dangerous, boundary for the people of the New Covenant. It was also an act that shattered other boundaries such as those of race, social status, and factions within the churches, and implied a willingness for a new constructed community and a new intimacy in Jesus. Sharing a cup, they had become blood brothers and sisters.

Does this call to drink from the one cup pose a challenge to contemporary Christian practice? It could be argued that sharing the cup is now common in some Catholic communities, but even where the cup is shared, it is interesting to see how many presbyters find reasons for avoiding it. Our hesitations to sharing a vessel that touches our lips are deep-seated. The Orthodox churches, for example, use a spoon—which destroys the gesture's force. Some Protestant churches use individual thimble-sized glasses that are as destructive of Jesus' bold symbolism as precut Catholic round wafers destroy the original loaf symbolism, while both transmit signals that appeal to our individualistic consumerist culture. While among Catholics, a severe flu season (much less a pandemic) causes the disappearance of the cup.

In every community the common cup is a source of contention in some way or other: and possibly that is the true value of this symbol in that it demands that each ask whether they can accept the implications of discipleship. Meanwhile, we rationalize these stresses with a mix of practicality, hygiene, and theology. In one tradition this will be the fear of "a spillage of the precious blood," in another it will be hygiene, while somewhere else it will be the time and awkwardness involved, or the problem of alcoholic wine . . . and the list—all with some factual basis—grows longer and longer. Likewise, groups develop subterfuges such as using a spoon or straws (*fistulae*), dipping ("intinction"), trays of mini-glasses; and, the most extreme deviation, making the cup individual to the president. These developments miss both the central imagery of the action and the shock that is at the gesture's core: will you share a cup and a common destiny in discipleship that might demand "obedience unto death" (see Phil 2:8)?

"Examine yourselves, and only then eat of the bread and drink of the cup" (1 Cor 11:28). Can we face the common cup of shared covenant discipleship?

A Community Action: The Size of the Group

We have all eaten of the one loaf and have drunk from the one cup, and our assembly is about to break up. There are just two more matters to think about: first, the collection of some money; and second, an announcement about next Saturday evening. The collection might seem a comedown from the spiritual heights of being united as a Christian family in the Spirit so that through, with, and in Jesus we might praise the Father and share his banquet, but the collection reminds us of our eucharistic context. We have shared in the divine banquet, we have rejoiced, and so we must be willing to share our goodness, our resources, our blessings with those in need. The collection is for the poor. I cannot love the God I cannot see and feast and ignore the poor person I can see who has not enough to eat. The line from the common table to the poor, from the banquet to the food bank, and from the society of the saints and angels to a more just society with living human beings must be direct and short. If the fruits of the Eucharist do not change our social environment, then they probably have not really changed us, and the liturgy has been but an elaborate drama.

Second, there is a natural human size to any meal gathering: usually only a handful can sit at a table, one can have a very large table for a special feast, but after a certain number we lose that intimacy that occurs only at a meal. We have been called to intimacy in being called by Jesus to his table, but in many places the size of the gathering is determined solely by the logistics of how many presbyters are available. So, our notice this evening might be that "Mass will be only in St. Matthew's next week" (a building on the other side of town), or "There will be no Mass next week because I am away and there is no cover available, but there will be a Communion Service led by Deacon Bill." And, alas, despite the best efforts of Deacon Bill, many will not really feel that there is much difference: readings, sermon, prayers, and Holy Communion—what is the fuss about?

It is worth recalling that the meals of the first Christians took place in their homes—it was an assembly that was small enough for everyone to know one another, for each to feel special, and for each to bring whatever special gifts they had to that community. It was a community, which then celebrated eucharist together. We still think and act in terms of a priest who celebrates and makes his services available as widely as possible, and the resulting group, no matter how many people are there or whether or not they have any sense of being

The hall in Berg Rothenfels (near Lohr on the river Main) in Germany was designed by Rudolf Schwarz so that it was a light-filled space to help a community to become self-aware and aware of the Mystery beyond images. Here Romano Guardini celebrated with groups of students in a space that caused them to focus on what they were doing as a group rather than on their surroundings. It is ecclesiology in action. Later, Karl Rahner remarked, "It is a widely known fact that the Rothenfels experience was the immediate model for the liturgical reforms of Vatican II."

known and belonging, is then simply called a community. Yet, not only in the early churches but for much of our history the experience of Christians was in tiny country parishes in which there would have been only a few dozen people present. Indeed, when we look at how to break up a loaf and arrange it on a dish, most of our evidence points to there being only about seventy people present (this practice died out because most no longer ate of the loaf). Likewise, the few surviving early medieval chalices have large cups that would be suitable for about the same number. We can see what these dishes (patens) and cups (chalices) looked like in the frescoes in San Vitale in Ravenna: on one side the emperor Justinian presents a dish at the Presentation of the Gifts, and on the other side, the empress presents the cup.

Our large, impersonal congregations forget the intimate size and personal involvement supposed by the nature of the Eucharist. Tackling this issue is probably the greatest reform challenge facing the Catholic Church today.

Chapter 5

The Banquet Story

We have neither groves nor altars.

—Minucius Felix

One cannot complete any book, much less a short book, on the Eucharist. There is always more to say, other avenues to explore, still more aspects of how we celebrate that call for careful attention. So rather than conclude, I want to leave you with an open vista that may generate your own questions.

As I write, I have just read an interview with Pope Francis (*La Civiltà Cattolica*, June 14, 2022) in which he says that resistance to the reforms of Vatican II is the major problem facing the Catholic Church today. He then said: "Restorationism has come to gag the Council. The number of groups of 'restorers'—for example, in the United States there are many—is significant." And nowhere is this truer than in relation to the Eucharist. Many people simply ignore our theology of the incarnation and deny that the reforms begun in Vatican II were and are desperately needed. They employ a series of false memories, combined with nostalgia and aestheticism, ignore the reality of what was done, along with the reasons, both theological and pastoral, for the reforms and the fact that such needed reforms could not be accomplished in a moment or even a decade, but are still in process.

A Greco-Roman period altar excavated in a Gentile house in Caesarea Philippi. Justin would have been familiar with altars like this because sacrifice was ubiquitous in his society. Christians had to distinguish their "sacrifice of praise" at their common table from such activities, while insisting that they, though ignoring altars, were not atheists. Even when Christians took over the language of altars and retained much of the Gentile understanding of sacrifice, their altar retained the basic form of a table.

In particular, I am always amazed by one argument repeated by those whom Pope Francis calls "the Restorers": that somehow the liturgy of 1970 was some sort of innovation "thought up in a moment" by a few trendy people—rather than the fruit of over a century of scholarship—and that somehow the "old rite" was the "ancient" one—rather than being an accidental jumble of bits and pieces that just became fossilized at various points in the Middle Ages. The best way to answer such criticisms is to read a genuine, very ancient text and ask two simple questions: do you recognize the reformed liturgy in this text? And does this text speak more of the reformed liturgy or that which it replaced?

The text comes from St. Justin, who was martyred in Rome around 165 CE. Although born in Samaria, near Nablus, he was a Gentile who became a convert to Christianity and then, writing in Greek, one of the great defenders of Christianity. In one of those works, known as the *First Apology*, he gave an account of the Eucharist—and it is one of our most precious liturgical monuments, allowing us to glimpse both how they celebrated the eucharistic meal and what it meant within their lives.

What Justin Wrote

First Apology, 13 [How Christians sacrifice and worship]

Could any sensible person call us "atheists"? We worship the Creator of this world and declare, as we have been taught, that he has no need of blood [-drenched sacrifices], libations, nor incense. We praise him to the best of our ability with a word of prayer and thanksgiving (*euché kai eucharistias*) for everything we eat. We have been taught that the only praise worthy of him is not that which consumes with fire what he has created for our sustenance, but to use them for our good and that of those in need; and then with thankful (*eucharistous*) voices to offer to him praises and hymns (*pompas kai humnous*) for our own creation, for keeping us in health, for the richness of life and the seasons, and to ask him in prayer that we come once more to incorruptible life because we have believed in him.

First Apology, 65 [What Christians do when a newly baptized person joins them]

After the washing of the one who has joined us, we take the person to where those we call "the brothers" have gathered to offer in common sincere prayers (*euchas*) for ourselves, for the person who has been enlightened, and for everyone else wherever they are. We do this so that, having found the truth, our actions might show us to be good citizens and observers of the law, and so attain to eternal salvation (*tén aiónion soterian*). The prayers ended, we greet one another with a kiss.

Then a loaf (*artos*) and a cup (*potérion*) containing water with some wine mixed into it (*hudati kekramenon*) are given to the person presiding over the brothers. He takes them and gives praise and glory to the Father of all through the name of the Son and of the Holy Spirit. He then gives, in the name of those to whom [God] has bestowed such favors, a worthy thanksgiving (*eucharistian*). When the prayers and the act of giving thanks (*euchas kai tén eucharistian*) are finished, all present, to declare their agreement, say "Amen." This is a Hebrew word meaning "may it be so."

And when the thanksgiving (*eucharistésantos*) of the presider has finished and the whole group (*laos*) has assented, those who, among us, are called "servants" (*diakonoi*) arrange for everyone to have a share (*metalabein*) of the loaf and wine and water of the thanksgiving (*tou eucharistéthentos*); and bring [shares] to those not present.

First Apology, 66–67 [Why Christians regularly assemble]

Among ourselves we call this food "eucharist" (*eucharistia*) and only those who have accepted the truth of our teachings and been cleansed of their sins and reborn by [baptism] and who order their lives by the Christ's teaching can share in it. The reason is that this is not an ordinary loaf or drink, but just as through God's word our savior Jesus Christ became flesh, taking our flesh and blood, for our salvation, so we have been instructed that the food over which we have prayed the thanksgiving is made by word the flesh and blood of that Jesus who was made flesh: this food is nourishment by which our flesh and blood are transformed.

The memoirs of the apostles (which we call "gospels") have transmitted to us what is enjoined on us. That Jesus took a loaf and, giving thanks (*eucharistésanta*), said "Do this in memory of me, this is my body." Similarly, he took the cup and, giving thanks, said "This is my blood" and gave it to them.

This is what the wicked demons have imitated when they commanded the same thing to be done in the mysteries of Mithras—for (as you either already know or else can easily discover) a loaf and a cup of water are used in their initiation rites.

Since then, we are constantly reminding each other of these things; and the wealthy among us help those who are poor; and we always stay together [*this sentence may have been displaced in the process of copying the text*]. Over everything that we have we bless (*eulogoumen*) him who made all things through his son, Jesus Christ, and the Holy Spirit.

First Apology, 67 [What Christians do at their gatherings]

Now on the day called "the day of the Sun" all who live in cities or in the country assemble in one place and the memoirs of the apostles or the writings of the prophets are read for as long as time allows. When the lector has stopped, the one presiding encourages us with words to imitate these good things [we have heard]. Then as a group we all stand up and offer our prayers.

And, as I have already mentioned, after our prayers are over, a loaf and wine and water (*oinos kai hudór*) are presented, and the presider offers prayers and thanksgiving (*euchas . . . kai eucharistias*) as best he can (*hosé dunamis*), and the assembly (*laos*) assent saying the "Amen."

Then there is distribution and each shares in those things over which there was the thanksgiving (*apo tón eucharistéthentón*), and they are taken by the "servants" (*diakonoi*) to those who are absent.

Then those who are wealthy, and willing, give whatever each thinks fit, and what is collected is left with the presider, who uses it to help widows and orphans and anyone

A human-sized space for a human-sized community, such as Justin would have known, with a table that speaks of "table-ness" and all that a table means to the baptized. It invites all to know one another and to stand side by side, in the presence of the risen Lord, around it. This Liturgy Room (in Carlow, Ireland, as it was in April 2015) was designed by Richard Hurley, inspired by Schwarz in Rotherfels, and was his attempt to help the assembly become "wholly celebrant."

else who is in need, be that due to sickness or some other problem, and also those among us who are slaves, or for strangers who are staying with us; in short, he cares for all those who are in need.

It is on the day of the Sun that all gather for our common assembly: because that is [for us] the first day—on which God, transforming the darkness and matter, made the universe; and on that day too our savior, Jesus Christ, rose from the dead. He was crucified on the day before the day of Saturn, and on the day after the day of Saturn, that is, the day of the Sun, he appeared to his apostles and disciples teaching them these things which we place before you for your consideration.

In another of his works, *The Dialogue with Trypho the Jew*, Justin gives this comment on the Eucharist which is a kind of summary of what he wanted to say and uses material from the Scriptures that would have been a common possession with Trypho.

The Dialogue with Trypho the Jew, 41 [The Christians' sacrifice of praise]

In a similar way, my friends, I continued, the cereal offering that those cleansed of leprosy were ordered to present [at the tent of meeting (see Lev 14:1-32, especially 10, 20-21, and 31)] was a prototype of the loaf of the thanksgiving (*tou artou tés eucharistias*) that our Lord, Jesus Christ, instructed us to offer in remembrance of the passion he suffered for all those souls who are cleansed of sin, in order that we should at the same time give thanks to God (*eucharistiómen tó theó*) for making the universe and everything in it for the sake of humanity, and for saving us from the sin in which we were born, and for the complete destruction of the evil powers and principalities through him who suffered in accordance with [God's] will.

Therefore, as I have already said, God speaks through the prophet Malachi, one of "the twelve" [minor prophets], regarding the sacrifices that are offered to himself:

I have no pleasure in you, says the Lord, and I will not accept an offering from your hands. For from the rising of the sun to its setting my name is great among the nations, and in every place incense is offered to my name, and a pure offering; for my name is great among the nations, says the Lord, but you profane it [Mal 1:10-12].

In making a reference to the sacrifices that we Gentiles offer to him in every place, that is, the loaf of thanksgiving (*tou artou tés eucharistias*), and, likewise, the cup of thanksgiving (*tou potériou . . . tés eucharistias*), he foretold that we should give glory to his name, but that you [Jews] should profane it.

The Dialogue with Trypho the Jew, 70 [That the actions of Jesus are prefigured in the Scriptures]

It is obvious that this prophecy [Isa 33:13-19] also alludes to the loaf that our Anointed One gave us to offer in remembrance of the body that he took for the sake of those who believe in him, for whom also he suffered, and, moreover, to the cup that he gave us as a remembrance of his blood when we are making thanksgiving (*eucharistountas poiein*).

The Dialogue with Trypho the Jew, 117 [The Christians' meal is the Christians' sacrifice]

God has declared in advance that all the sacrifices offered in his name that Jesus Christ commanded us to offer, that is, the thanksgiving of the loaf and the cup (*eucharistia tou artou kai tou potériou*) that we Christians offer in every place, are pleasing to him. But, by contrast, he refuses to accept your sacrifices offered through your priests, as he says:

and I will not accept an offering from your hands. For from the rising of the sun to its setting my name is great among the nations . . . but you profane it [Mal 1:10-12].

. . . [Justin continues his attack on Jewish practices] . . .

I accept that the prayers and thanksgivings (*euchai kai eucharistiai*) of worthy people are the only perfect and acceptable sacrifices to God. Christians, therefore, have received a tradition that they are to make only such sacrifices in the recollection they make for their food, whether solid or liquid, and in which the sufferings of the Son of God are remembered.

In Justin we hear someone who has that freshness about worship and liturgy that is rare in any time but here is given added vibrancy because he was both a great teacher and one for whom these were, literally, matters of ultimate concern. His writings, especially his *First Apology* 65–67, have inspired many down the centuries who have sought a more authentic liturgy—and the passage has even become a liturgical text as the second reading in the Office of Readings of the Third Sunday of Easter. When his feast comes around, June 1, invoke him as the patron of our continual need to make our worship both fitting and more real.

And finally, . . .

Can we express our living unity with this faith of ancient times in a Tweet? Here is my attempt:

Assemble the disciples
Relive the memories
Bless the Father
Break the loaf
Drink the cup
Share our riches
Look forward to the Banquet.

Scripture Index

Subject Index